SOMETIMES, CHURCH HURTS

Blessings

Danny Cheney

Sometimes, Church Hurts
By Danny Cheney

Copyright © 2015 by Danny Cheney.

Cover photograph by Robert Hafley

Some names have been changed to protect the identity of those involved.

Special thanks to Velma Reed for her help in editing this project.

This book is dedicated to Sonya, my wife and partner in ministry. She has walked every step with me in our journey to heal divided churches. The road we have travelled has not been easy, but she has done it with grace and strength.

Contents

INTRODUCTION

Hanging in my office is a painting I inherited from my grandfather. It is an obscure piece of art that I can find nothing about the picture nor the artist. Pablo Valero painted this masterpiece that hangs above my computer desk. Centered on the canvas is a white lamb with arrows piercing him all over. Blood is dripping from its body which creates a pool on the ground beneath. In small letters on each arrow are written a variety of sins. There are different things that tragically affect Christ's church: envy, petty-mindedness, sensitivity, false accusations, unjustified criticism, spite, revenge, impatience, vindictiveness, insincerity, and conclusions without facts. There are many more sins written that pierced this lamb, but it is the words written on the top and on the bottom that truly tell the tale.

At the top, it quotes a portion of John 1:29, "Behold the Lamb of God." The lamb in this picture is none other than Jesus Christ. What is written on the bottom gives us insight into what these sins do to the Lamb of God. It reads from *Zechariah 13:6, "I was wounded in the house of my friends."* Therefore, every arrow that pierces someone in the body of Christ, pierces our Savior. When we hurt, He hurts.

Just like Jesus was wounded in the House of His friends, so it is with us as believers. We, too, can be wounded in the House of God. Every sin mentioned above is a real threat to each one of us and many times it comes from our closest relationships.

I would love to know the story behind Pablo Valero's painting and how he came up with each of the sins labeled on the arrows. Something deep inside me says that he has a story; that somewhere, he faced many of these things in his own life. There is an inscription at the bottom of this picture that reveals that it was promoted by a large denominational association. It is a real possibility that what is painted in this picture is the result of hurts that had been received at the hands of other believers. It happens and this is why you hold this book in your hands.

When I began in ministry, I had dreams of pastoring being simple and easy. I get to preach and pray. What an awesome job! Doing what God has called me to do. I wasn't saved until I was nineteen and even though I attended church most of my life, I never paid attention to anything in church. I didn't know the "inside story".

I embarked on my pastoral journey when I was twenty-four. I had the privilege to pastor a small congregation in a little southeast Texas country town, but I had no idea how to pastor a church. I didn't go to bible college, nor did I have a long legacy of ministry in my family from which to learn the tricks of the trade.

I learned two ways: from my mistakes and by the Holy Spirit. I tried to follow His leading but much of my experience came from trial and error, and let's face it, just plain being thrown in the middle of a mess. When a pastor looks into a calling to a church, the church generally never divulges the history or the conflict. I have found that pastors doctor up their resumes to make themselves look good and churches tend to do the same. Pastors want a church and churches want a pastor.

I tell you this because I never looked for the opportunity to go to a troubled church but God allowed me to and I am thankful to have been used by Him in the healing process. Nearly two decades later, I look back on our ministry in four churches and have fond memories of congregations that have found healing from the wounds caused by other believers.

All four churches that we have pastored, at different times, had various struggles and not every situation was the same. In every church there was a common denominator - conflict. People don't always get along with one another. While, many church hurts are not intentional, they are often responses to our own pain. Some things that happen in a congregation are just indications of deeper problems in the church or in individual lives. The wounds of God's house are sometimes at the hand of clergy, while other times, it is at the hand of laypeople. Regrettably, innocent bystanders are caught in the cross-fire and they experience church like they never thought possible.

Over the years, my wife and I have learned quite a few things about putting the pieces back together again. We didn't enter these situations as experts coming in to fix the problem. We entered blindly without knowledge of the full scale of what went on before we arrived. In the course of our ministry, though, we have learned that God's Word has all the answers to dealing with these issues. There are principles that God has given in

His Word that, if followed, will bring tremendous victory and healing to those who are wounded in the House of God. God's Word transcends across any boundary and can be used effectively in every church in every place. God's Word is not just for a particular situation. It is the answer for all things.

In the pages of this book, there are some very pointed issues that are dealt with. I challenge you to read with an open heart and an open mind. Often, the hurts cannot be healed unless we search the core of our own hearts. Allow God to open you like a book and read the pages of your heart. When you agree to that, you make yourself available to be healed of the wounds that afflict you.

No matter where you have been, or what you have faced, God has a healing for your heart and I know you will find it! As you read this, you will discover that what you have experienced is normal. Honestly, I have come to realize that *Sometimes, Church Hurts.*

1

GOD'S GREAT CHURCH

In 1991, I answered God's call. It was a call that was real and distinct and I can still take you to that place and show you how it happened. Never had I heard God speak to me as clear as He did that day. It was a holy moment!

My wife, Sonya, was working that evening so I decided to spend some time in prayer. I had only been a believer for several months and I wanted more of God in my life. Never had the thought of ministry entered my mind. I just wanted to serve the Lord any way I could, but preaching wasn't something that I considered my call.

That night as I prayed, I heard within my heart the voice of God for the first time of my young Christian life. It was clear and precise. God simply said, "I want you to preach my Gospel." That was it. Nothing more but certainly nothing less. Instantly, I felt an unction to preach the

things, the church struggles. The church will face opposition, not from without, but from within.

The Word of God is clear that when we are on God's true mission, persecution will come. Truth is never swallowed easily and so it will create tension with the world around us. Therefore, that persecution doesn't come from within the church. It comes from the outside, but when our eyes start to be centered on our own needs and wants within Christ's body, church becomes a place of disunity, friction and hurt. Here is where my burden lies.

My deep love for God's church and the unity of the believers drives me. I believe my heart is shared with the heart of God. This very thing is displayed in the writings of the apostles. They wanted unity and knew this was the only way to see a move of God. Unity was the only way that God's great church could stand. The main way that the church can withstand pressure from the outside is that it remains strong from the inside. The apostles understood this principle and promoted harmony in the body of Christ.

There is no greater display of the burden of the apostles than the great man of God, Paul. He was saved from a religious background. He was known as the Pharisee of all Pharisees. In fact, he was the persecutor of the church from the outside. It was Paul who sought to destroy God's church, but he couldn't do it. The church was too strong within to be torn down from the outside.

Finally, Paul encountered the Messiah and became a follower of Christ. His life radically changed. He was called to preach and teach the Gospel and he went all in. Paul became the greatest of all apostles. He went on to write two thirds of the New Testament before he was martyred. He, too, had a burden for God's great church.

Paul had suffered much for the sake of the Gospel. Throughout his life, he endured hardships that most of us will never face. Yet, he remained steadfast. In his writing to the Corinthians, the Apostle Paul shared about the burdens that he had borne:

II Corinthians 11:23-28, "in labors more abundant, in stripes above measure, in prisons more frequently, in deaths often. 24 From the Jews five times I received forty stripes minus one. 25 Three times I was beaten with rods; once I was stoned; three times I was shipwrecked; a night and a day I have been in the deep; 26 in journeys often, in perils of waters, in perils of robbers, in perils of my own countrymen, in perils of the Gentiles, in perils in the city, in perils in the wilderness, in perils in the sea, in perils among false brethren; [27] *in weariness and toil, in sleeplessness often, in hunger and thirst, in fastings often, in cold and nakedness—* [28] *besides the other things, what comes upon me daily: my deep concern for all the churches."*

This list of things that Paul had faced reveals the immense suffering that he had dealt with for the Gospel's sake. However, there is one phrase that arrests my attention, *"besides the other things, what comes upon me daily: my deep concern for all the churches."* What I glean from this is that Paul is saying, "The suffering I faced physically is nothing compared to the concern I have for these churches." In essence, he is saying that his burden for the church is far greater than any physical suffering.

Why would Paul take this approach? Because he understood that the church was the agent that would change the world. The church has the responsibility to lift up Jesus Christ and make Him known but this is where we often fail. Paul understood what was at stake here. Our mission can be compromised when we do not focus on what we know is God's call for His people. Paul was burdened for the churches he had charge of because he knew that people can veer off on the wrong path.

The early church was facing, not only persecution, but false teachers had cropped up in the body seeking to lead people astray with a contrary gospel. Already in the Corinthian church, division had set in. Although it might seem noble, some were followers of Peter, some Apollos and some followed after Paul. Personalities were driving the church, when the number one personality, Jesus Christ was being missed. The church was only a few decades old and already division was evident. Paul was driven by this concern. This is why he addressed it in his letters to these churches.

Yet, despite all that, God's great church is still alive. It is still a living organism making an impact some nearly 2,000 years later. It is a testimony to what Jesus said, "The gates of Hell shall not prevail against My church." The reason we are still alive is because God's Spirit is still alive and is raising up a people who are still concerned about seeing His church make an impact. This is my burden.

Though the church is still going forward, there are some churches that are barely hanging on to life. The issues of division and church hurts have become so real that people leave with open wounds and the church suffers. I have witnessed it with my own eyes. I have watched as people walk away from a church they knew for 50 years having to start over because they can't bear the pain any longer.

God's great church will press on. It will never die and it is still worth the risk of us being vulnerable to hurt. The problem is not with God but rather with flawed people. We have a large section of books in every Christian bookstore on how to get along with your spouse and children, and how to build strong families. Yet, the largest, most diverse family we know has very few books about how to get along. There should be books discussing how the Family of God is to get along. There should be a section in the bookstore on how to take God's great church and make it stronger through trust and relationships.

I have heard it said for many years, "Strong families make strong churches." But I have found that we can have strong families in churches that do not get along with other strong families. Yes, we must focus on the family; however, we must also emphasize building strong relationships in the Body of Christ.

In our generation, we don't need another

theological reformation; we need a reformation of love for one another and strong relationships. We need to focus on Christ's mission and lay aside our differences. The church's greatest days are ahead. I believe there is a new reformation on the way, a reformation of a unified church impacting the world for Jesus Christ. Will you be a part of this great movement? The church of Jesus Christ is this world's greatest hope.

Before we dive into some pretty heavy discussions, I want you to take a moment to pray that God would grant you open ears and an open heart to this message. The language can be tough at times, but please understand the burden of my heart. It is not meant in anyway to be critical or harsh. I have a passion to see us build a church that will be without spot or wrinkle so that when Christ comes, He will receive His glorious church.

2

NEEDLESS CASUALTIES

I remember well my first few months as the pastor of a church that had recently split. It was one of those life-changing moments in my ministry and helped me understand the pain of church hurts.

One Sunday night there was a defining moment for us as a church. I had preached a message the Lord had laid on my heart about forgiving others who have hurt you, even those who have hurt you in the House of God. For a church that had voted the former pastor out and had seen two factions form in the aftermath, the message hit home. I addressed those who were for the former pastor and those who were against. The message was the same to both crowds. Forgive and love. Something clicked in the hearts of people that night and we seemed to have a breakthrough service. I truly thought we had won a victory.

At eight o'clock the next morning I received a phone call. It was from a young couple in the church who had attended for many years. The young man's grandmother had helped found the church and his family had a rich history in this congregation. They were calling to ask to meet with me that afternoon. I generally get nervous when a couple wants to meet that quickly and is willing to take off from their jobs. This time was no different.

Again, I had only recently assumed the pastorate of this troubled church. I didn't know who was on what side and I certainly couldn't determine who was friend or foe.

When they arrived at my office, the conversation started quickly. The wife spoke up and said, "What you preached about last night is impossible! There is too much hurt here. This has been going on for years and the pastor getting voted out was the final straw. We have seen so much in our years here that there is no way we can forgive. It is impossible to get over it this time."

Those words haunted me. There is no way to forgive? It is impossible to get over it? The church is meant to be a safe haven, a place of rest and refuge. Yet, this young couple was betrayed and wounded. The pain was more than they could bear.

There are times when a pastor knows that so much damage has been done that the only option is for their parishioners to find another place to worship and to find healing. This young couple picked up a lifetime of memories and started their church journey over in another congregation. The decision for them had become easy. They were meeting with me to let me know that they were done with the hurt this church had brought them.

All too often this is the picture that is painted in the modern day church. A church that is divided. A church that is wrecked by people who seem to be so spiritual but are actually lethal weapons. In my grandfather's old Bible, he wrote in the margins about Christians who had been hurt in church. He called them "needless casualties of war." Sadly, there are many of these casualties in today's church, or worse yet, they have dropped out of church.

The Bible tells us that the gates of Hell shall not prevail against the church and that is true, the gates of Hell will not prevail. The church, however, can destroy itself from within.

The enemy of our souls has raised an attack against the greatest institution that was ever created: The Church of Jesus Christ. God intended that this organism change the world, but instead the enemy has sown discord into the body. It is a cancer that spreads rapidly. It is a disease that will nag the body for years to come.

Paul, in writing to the Corinthian believers, addressed the seriousness of Satan's attack on the church. He revealed that the enemy will use unforgiveness to destroy the work of God.

II Corinthians 2:10-11 says, "Now whom you forgive anything, I also forgive. For if indeed I have forgiven anything, I have forgiven that one for your sakes in the presence of Christ, lest Satan should take advantage of us; for we are not ignorant of his devices."

Satan has done a great job of taking advantage of God's people. He has robbed them of their joy and sowed seeds of bitterness. The sad thing is we *are* ignorant of his devices. He goes undetected through the body of Christ, hurting, wounding, lying and killing the spirits of mature and seasoned believers. Many of these wounded Christians never recover from their hurts. Unless

God's people come together and let the healing begin, many churches will die.

Jesus said a house divided against itself cannot stand. There are a lot of churches that have divided, and with that division, comes needless casualties. These casualties maim and wound people for life. Maybe you are one of those. I was a casualty at one time.

It is interesting to me that this is a problem of major proportions. The majority of churches in the United States are under 150 people. They are small churches by number and most will never grow because of the casualties they produce.

On the inside of a beautiful structure you would hope to find a group of genuine believers who will love you as you are. The truth is, however, that in many churches there are schisms that destroy the life of the church. God's anointing cannot abide in a divided church.

The church today has produced a group of people who have been wounded in the house of God. They didn't ask for what they received. It may have come from a pastor or minister of the church, or it may have come from another believer. Nevertheless, they become casualties because of something that was said or done to hurt them.

"Let them leave the church. Good-riddens. They shouldn't wear their feelings on their shoulders." This is the attitude that they receive from the body of Christ. Some remain in the church hanging onto their hurts only to find salt being poured into their open wounds. Why must this be?

What unfolds in the chapters to follow are the necessary parts to be healed of your wounds. Whether it was your pastor who hurt you or a fellow believer, my prayer is that you will find healing for your wounded soul. You do not have to live like this. God has much more for you!

3

LIFE IS NOT ALWAYS FAIR

Life's not fair, is it? Definitely not and we don't always get what we deserve. Thus is my experience in dealing with people. It is often those who are closest to us that hurt us the most. Many times, the very ones that you have blessed in some way are the ones that wound you.

Why is it that we are hurt by these "friends"? It is because we make ourselves vulnerable to those who we are close to. We are more vulnerable to those we TRUST. This doesn't mean we should never trust again; in fact, you MUST trust again. We will discuss this in a later chapter.

I have never understood why Christians could be so hurtful but I am learning that most Christians who are the offenders were at one time a victim. Let me explain. The ones who hurt you have probably been wounded a time or two in the past. They may not even intentionally hurt you; it just may be their reaction to their own hurts.

What I have witnessed over the years of pastoring churches with hurting people is that people respond differently to hurt. Some have an easier time overcoming these wounds than others do. Many, however, will lash out at you in fear of being hurt again, and there lies the problem. Because of this, the wounded saint will often turn around and hurt someone else.

Hopefully, this makes sense to you. I challenge you to look past the scathing remarks or the harsh criticism you have received and look at that person's life to see if he or she needs healing, too.

If you are in a close relationship long enough, you will see that even our friends can be channels of pain. Such is the case within the church. As a body of believers it is necessary that we build strong relationships with fellow Christians. It is the hallmark of a New Testament church to have fellowship with each other. Yet, at times, today's church will have division with those we fellowship with.

Many years ago, I had a dear friend whom I highly admired more than any other person. He had become a spiritual father to me. We thought alike and we shared the same desires and the same heart for God's Kingdom. One day we had a major disagreement, which can be common among friends. Disagreements should never destroy friendships because friendships allow for individual opinions. I didn't know that this argument would ruin a marvelous friendship. It is too long a story to go into detail about, but the discussion never became heated and it appeared we left with a mutual understanding. That evening at church, my friend would not speak to me. He avoided me like the plague and it seemed as if he cared nothing about our friendship. I was deeply wounded by that experience.

We have reconciled today but our friendship has never returned to what it was before. I realize that I was at fault in why we had the disagreement, but I never intended that it would ruin a friendship. Both my friend and I share a heart that has been wounded by the other. The experience I had with my friend broke my heart. It was a friendship as Jonathan and David had in the Old Testament. We were spiritual brothers. I was there when he needed a friend and he was there when I needed a friend. We shared moments of joy and we shared each other's pain. I was deeply saddened when it ended so abruptly.

King David experienced the same type of

relational problems. Psalm 35 paints an incredible picture of a heart that had been wounded by what seemed to be friends.

Psalm 35:11-14, "Fierce witnesses rise up: they ask me things that I do not know. They reward me evil for good, to the sorrow of my soul. But as for me, when they were sick, my clothing was sackcloth; I humbled myself in fasting; and my prayer would return to my own heart. I paced about as though he were my friend or brother; I bowed down heavily as one who mourns for his mother."

David recollects how he had been treated by those that he had dealt with fairly. Those who persecuted him and turned against him were the very ones that he had ministered to and prayed for. They were the ones that he mourned and fasted for as if they were his family.

Then all of a sudden, they turned their backs on him, not caring about his feelings or his hurt. David was dealt with unjustly and maybe you have been too. Many people wear the same shoes that David did. They feel the hurt of a relationship gone bad. Looking at the relationship now with hindsight I am sure you could see some warning signs but you were still a true friend.

You should always endeavor to be a true friend even if the favor is not returned. You must always seek to be a blessing even when you aren't blessed in return. We are to always be a caring person even if we do not feel cared for. This is the mark of a believer, always loving even if it is not returned. The ones who hurt you may think nothing of the pain they have caused but you should still love them.

David would not touch King Saul even when he had the chance for revenge. When David had the opportunity to kill the traitor, Absalom, he refrained and instead extended his love. Friend, that is being the better man. You might ask, "Even when they keep pouring salt on my open wounds?" The Word of God's answer is "yes."

David continued the Psalm by saying, "but in my adversity they rejoiced and gathered together; Attackers gathered against me, and I did not know it; they tore at me and did not cease; with ungodly mockers at feasts they gnashed at me with their teeth." (Psalm 35:15-16)

Thank God I have never experienced a friendship gone as badly as David's but I have witnessed many that have. These so called friends were now rejoicing when David was living in adversity. They forgot his acts of kindness. They failed to remember his times of fasting and prayer for their healing. Many friends are only your friends when they need you. Such was the case with David.

Friendships should always be give and take but often it is only take for some people. David found that these friends had become fierce foes. One way to determine a true friend is one that will rejoice while you are being blessed even though that person is walking in poverty.

A true friend will be your friend no matter what. If you are his or her friend while you both walk in adversity and one day you seem to get blessed beyond measure, that person should be happy for you. Many friends find this cause to be jealous.

Jealousy in relationships is probably one of the top causes of division. Envy is a tool of the enemy to divide the church and especially to divide the clergy. This is where Satan appeals to man's pride. We want to be the best. We want to be blessed. We want to be the one to receive the glory. Jealousy can destroy friendships.

When you are hurt, you feel debilitated and stunned and it might take a while to get over the wounds of a friend who has hurt you. We need to be as David. We need to make sure that we do not become bitter by the wounds of those who call themselves believers.

Let me put it very plainly. If you go to church regularly and build relationships with other believers, you will be hurt at some time or another. I would like to candy coat this for you and make you feel better BUT it is the truth. You see, the fallibilities of Christian friends will help you draw closer to God. He is the only one who will never hurt you.

There are two ways for you to keep your focus on God during hurtful church experiences:

Pray for God to touch you.

David said, "Lord, how long will You look on? Rescue me from their destructions."

When you are hurt don't lash back. Pray that God would rescue you from the pain and help mend your broken heart. Your pain can only be mended by God Almighty. Even if you are reconciled with your brother or sister in Christ you will still have the scars of a major wound that doesn't heal easily. You have to count on God to bind up your broken heart.

Praise The Mender.

David also said, "I will give You thanks in the assembly; I will praise You among many people."

It is easy to sit back and throw in your spiritual towel and say I am never going to church again. The other way to do it is just praise God that He never changes nor hurts you. By lifting up His name, he will lift you up. If you are hurting on the inside, just begin to worship the Friend who sticks closer than a brother. It will help heal your wounds.

What we get in life is not always what we want or even what we deserve but we can be sure that God is always on our side. Life isn't fair; that is what makes heaven so grand. As believers we cannot allow our hurts to destroy us. Most of all we should endeavor not to be the one who hurts others.

4

CHRISTIANS KILL THEIR WOUNDED

In the early 1970's in a small town on the Texas coast a pastor I knew well experienced malicious Christians first hand. He was a hard preacher who preached a great deal against sin. Some people cannot handle when a preacher talks about gossip, backbiting, and sexual sin in the church. This pastor, however, would not compromise.

One day he came home to find one of his board members waiting for him, with a moving truck, and informed him that he had until dark to get out. The church had all they could take of this nosy preacher. They forced him out of town and told him never to return.

This sounds like an old western that says "this town ain't big enough for the two of us" but it is a true story. This pastor shared with me later a statement that I have never forgotten. He said,

"Christians kill their wounded."

Christians kill their wounded? Isn't the body of Christ meant to be a support system? Not all church people are like those in that small town but there are some believers that have no qualms about lashing out at others.

Look at your community on a Sunday morning and you will find a host of people who were once church going folks but now have resigned to the label of the unchurched. Why? Because they have been wounded in the house of God. The truth is, in the church there is enough carnality to give the world a run for its money. "Christians" can be vicious.

In fact, in my research on the subject, I was amazed to find the reaction of those who had been through church problems. One lady who had been through a church split said, "I was saddened by the loss of membership and people I had known all my life leaving the church. Apparently, a lot of the people who left our church did not stay with the new church group and others moved from church to church, never satisfied, or backslid." People backslid over church problems? What a pity that disagreements would drive people away from the things of the Lord! Multiply that by the thousands and we will see the reality of those who have been wounded and fell away from the faith.

When I pastored my first church in a small Texas town, a lady was in our church who didn't have a problem with expressing her negative opinions. One Sunday morning all through the service as I was ministering and preaching, this lady was staring me down. If looks could kill, I would be six-foot under. I don't know if it quenched the Spirit but it sure quenched mine.

During that service there was a young man visiting that I knew needed Jesus. At the altar call he came down and we prayed for him but he did not receive Christ. After the altar time he returned to his seat which was directly behind this disgruntled lady's pew. I closed the service and I made my way to the back to greet people.

I noticed her looking at me again with anger in her eyes so I approached her. The young man was still seated behind her when I asked, "Mary, is everything all right this morning?"

She said in a hateful response, "No! I am mad at you!"

I glanced to look at the young man and his eyes became as wide as saucers. He quickly left the building and never returned. He witnessed firsthand the carnality that is found in many

Christians. Only God knows what will become of his eternal state.

In writing to Timothy, Paul commends him for his GENUINE faith. Genuine means sincere, without hypocrisy. Are you genuine? Child of God, it is not becoming of a believer to become entangled in the web of church discord. Discord is labeled as one of the things God hates. Discord, however, has become a fruit of many modern day churches.

In church there are many different personalities. There are those who are strong-willed and those who are meek. There are the introverts and the extroverts. There are leaders and then there are followers. God created different personality types because He can use all people and these personalities have their place in the Kingdom of God.

The problem lies in the fact that people do not know how to get along with those who are opposite of them. We have a tendency to want everyone to be like us. If someone irritates us, we let them know about it. If we feel like we are wronged, we blow up. This is not the way it is supposed to be.

Many people are bearing hurts from past wounds and they react to others because of those hurts. Most who are guilty of hurting others have at one time or another been a victim. They react the way they feel is right. This is not an excuse for them. It is just a matter of what they know to do.

Therefore, we must learn how to get along with each other and display the Fruits of the Spirit. If every Christian would exercise and bear the Fruits of the Spirit, the church would be unified and healthy. God has given each believer these fruits to use at their disposal. The book of Galatians describes the Fruit of the Spirit. In these fruits we can find some traits that will help us in our dealings with other people. The fruits that we need are as follow:

Love

Love we will discuss in a later chapter but let's look at the definition. The Greek word for love in Galatians five is Agape which means an undefeatable benevolence and unconquerable good will that seeks the highest good of the other person, no matter what he does. We are to love everyone whether he or she deserves it or not.

Longsuffering

Let's face it. Some people can steadily get on your nerves. The easiest thing for us to do is lash back and hurt them. Longsuffering , however, guides to be PATIENT. I know you are wondering why I had to bring that up. Who likes patience? But longsuffering will help you deal with people that are not easy to get along with.

The word longsuffering means having patience, bearing suffering a long time, having perseverance, being constant, being steadfast and enduring. It is a trait that will help you deal with people and continue to love them and that love will never wear thin.

Years ago, I experienced the worst of days. I came home after a tough day at the office and I wanted to be left alone. Such is not the case in the house with a seven-year-old boy. Everything he did that day got on my nerves. I would gripe at him and get onto him for every little thing. I looked at the hurt in his eyes when God spoke to my heart and said, "Danny, aren't you glad that I am more patient with you." Aren't you glad that God is longsuffering in His dealings with us?

The Psalmist says it the best, "If You, Lord, should mark iniquities, O Lord, who could stand?" (Psalm 130:3)

We should try to be as longsuffering as God is.

People are human and they mess up. We should have longsuffering towards them just as God does.

Kindness

There are some people that you look at and they display kindness. These are the people that I love to deal with. They are always able to handle any situation with gentleness and love. In fact the word kindness literally means gentleness in dealing with others.

This is not a trait that is meant for someone else. It is a trait that is meant for you and me. Each believer is supposed to walk in kindness.

Gentleness

Have you ever seen a guy who is six foot five and 250 pounds of muscles and someone says, "Oh, he's just a big teddy bear." He may look intimidating but he is actually a gentle person. We should all be gentle. The Fruit of the Spirit, Gentleness, means a disposition that is even-tempered, balanced in Spirit, and having our passions under control.

It is hard to find balanced people today but a gentle person is one who is even tempered and balanced in spirit. It is like a dog that is found in the house of a six-year-old that can take abuse and never bite the kid. As believers we are to be even-tempered, not easily provoked.

Self-Control

Paul says that we are to have self-control in all things including our dealings with other people. It is a natural instinct to blow our top when someone makes us mad. However, it is a display of our maturity in Christ if we can control our temper. Self-control is the ability to suppress your fleshly desire to blow up.

All believers should display these fruits in their lives. If all believers would make these things evident in their lives, the church would have unity and a spirit of love. It is possible! The early church had all things in common and were in one mind in one accord.

The church today wants to operate in the gifts of the Spirit while they throw the fruits of the Spirit right out the window. Friends, God expects believers to be genuine in their faith, without hypocrisy.

A church is supposed to be a safe haven for unbelievers but when there is contention among God's people the lost cannot see any hope. My prayer for every church is that they will lay aside all of their differences and focus on the commission of the church not the faults of others. It should never be that Christians kill their wounded but instead should bind up the brokenhearted.

5

SPIRITUAL WARFARE

Since Satan fell from Heaven, he has tried to thwart God's plan. He tempted Adam and Eve in the Garden of Eden and they fell into sin. It seemed he had conquered mankind. It was a plan of enormous consequences. Man was now a sinful being and the enemy had a foothold on God's creation.

Ever since that day, Satan has tried to come against God's chosen people. He plotted against the Jews in the Old Testament. He tempted Jesus in the Gospels. The church of Acts would be his target after the resurrection. Today, the church of Jesus Christ is the focus of Satan's plan to cripple God's purpose once again.

Jesus said, "The gates of Hell would not prevail against His church." Thank God He gave us hope, but we often overlook one detail in this verse.

Even if the gates of Hell will not prevail against us, it still means that we are in a war. If the devil weren't fighting, Jesus would have no need to give us the promise of victory.

The war that we are waging is not an external war against the forces of evil in the world, as much as it is an internal war. It is a battle that rages deep inside the church. It is a war between believers. You might label it a civil war in the church. Believers who are involved are not necessarily emissaries for the devil. They may not even realize they are being used, but Satan can infuse certain things in believers and they can act them out. Satan's strategy is ingenious. It is a battle plan that Jesus Himself said was a sure means of victory.

"Every kingdom divided against itself is brought to desolation, and every city or house divided against itself will not stand." Matthew 12:25

If the church is divided, it will not grow. If there is a division, we will not be the force God intended us to be. The reality of this is that if the people of God do not stand up and refuse to be divided, the church will decline.

The early church was in one mind and one

accord but that doesn't mean that they never had disagreements. Satan tried to bring opposition within the church and even to the apostles, but he did not prevail. Friend, every church will have problems arise. It is how we deal with those problems, that counts.

The greatest example of dissension in the early church came in Acts chapter six. "Now in those days, when the number of the disciples was multiplying, there arose a complaint." Acts 6:1. The church had grown to over 8,000 people in a matter of months and should we be shocked to think there would be hiccups in the process. Our thoughts often tend to be that if we are in the perfect will of God nothing will go wrong. As if Satan is sitting around saying, "O goodness, that church sure has grown fast. I can't believe it. Good luck to them. I wish them the best." Have we forgotten that Satan is our adversary? Our enemy? The truth is, he isn't sitting around wondering what he will do. He is standing up and saying, "I will get them to focus on themselves and start complaining. Division will come and I will prevail against them."

In the early church, a complaint arose. This is possibly the greatest stress factor of today's pastors. There arose a complaint. Complaints are contagious. They tend to find a group of people who feel the same way as they do but they haven't said anything yet. Complaining is the enemy's tool of stopping the momentum of a growing church.

What we find in this story is a group of believers who have started being more concerned about themselves than they are about the growth of the church. The devil has deceived the church into becoming a consumer society rather than a catalyst to change the world. This becomes evident in the rest of Acts chapter six verse one.

"There arose a complaint against the Hebrews by the Hellenists, because their widows were neglected in the daily distribution."

Did you notice something significant in this verse? The Hellenists were a group of people. The complaint was not an isolated disgruntled church member who had voiced his or her concern to the apostles. This was a group of people who were upset with another group. The Hebrews were being treated better in the church than the Hellenists were, so they thought.

The Hebrews were natives of Israel and spoke Hebrew (or Aramaic) rather than Greek. The

Hellenists were Jews who were natives of the Greco-Roman world and spoke Greek. *(Spirit Filled Life Bible Notes)* There was obviously some dissension between the two people groups about who was more accepted within the growing church.

This book deals with finding healing from church hurts but I must interject that some hurts come because we have our own view of what we think is right and how we should be treated within the church. The enemy has brought division in the body of Christ through well-meaning people who feel that they aren't being treated fairly. There is a spirit of offense that has been unleashed upon the church.

In the last decade I have seen this spirit multiplied in the body of Christ. People are offended by everything that is done in the church, from wanting to change the color of the carpet to the accusation of showing favorites or from not showing enough concern for one people group to showing too much concern for another. I believe the enemy has unleashed a spirit of offense that seeks to divide and cause a division that is beyond repair.

"A brother offended is harder to win than a strong city, and contentions are like the bars of a castle."

Proverbs 18:19

Simply put, the spirit of offense is the ability to get offended easily over little things. If things don't go your way do you get mad and hurt over it? If your church changes something and you don't like it, do you find yourself wanting to leave? Are you easily offended over things other people say? My encouragement to every believer is to get on your face before God and ask Him if you are bearing a spirit of offense.

It is time we go to war against Satan. It is time, as the people of God, that we do not wear our feelings on our shoulders anymore. There are many legitimate hurts that people experience in church, but we cannot allow those hurts to destroy the church or us as individuals. The apostles took those complaints and created a plan to overcome them.

The scenario today is altogether different than the early church. There are many churches attend. If we get upset in our church, we can go down the road and find a better one. Could this be the reason the body of Christ might appear unstable today? Satan has given us magnifying glasses to help expose the faults in other individuals and churches. We truly are pulling the splinter from someone else's eye while looking around the log in our own eye.

The only way the early church overcame offenses was through keeping their focus on the purpose of the church. They had problems just like today's church. Read the book of First Corinthians and you will see what the Apostle Paul had to deal with. One group liked Apollos' preaching better than Paul's. Another group had divided because they held to Peter's teachings and it was their way or the highway.

It was Paul who wrote, "Now I plead with you, brethren, by the name of our Lord Jesus Christ, speak the same thing and that there be no divisions among you, but that you be perfectly joined together in the same mind and in the same judgment." I Corinthians 1:10

This is the message for today's church. He is not addressing the different denominations or religions. Paul is addressing different groups of people who had formed within the Corinthian church. If they did not begin to speak the same thing, they would have lost the church. So it is for us today. If we do not all speak the same thing, the church cannot survive and Satan knows this.

*"Now whom you forgive anything, I also forgive.
For if indeed I have forgiven anything , I have forgiven
that one for your sakes in the presence of Christ, lest
Satan should take advantage of us; for we are not
ignorant of his devices." II Corinthians 2:10-11*

Paul is again writing to the Corinthian church.
They had been divided over many issues. He tells
them that they must walk in forgiveness lest they
fall into Satan's snare. Did you notice that?
Division is one of Satan's snares and again, it is
how you go through it that determines the
outcome. Forgiveness is the key! Overlooking
transgression and faults is the key to overcoming
division. Casting off the spirit of offense keeps the
church from division. Satan takes advantage of us
in this area, but unlike the Corinthians, we seem
to be ignorant of his devices.

We have not attributed our hurts to the enemy.
We have associated the problems we face with
either God or his church. It is the enemy who
wants to destroy you. It is not God who hurts you
to the point that you want to leave the church. It is
not God that makes you bitter and want to walk
away from Him. Do not be ignorant of Satan's
devices. We are living in the last days and the

enemy is trying to destroy God's people. If the devil can succeed at that, he will destroy the church.

You are not reading this book by accident! God is going to help you to overcome your hurts and give you the spirit of love in the place of offense. Friend, let's serve the devil notice together that we will not stand and take his abuse anymore. Your eyes have been opened to what has been taking place in your life. Your hurts are going to be healed and the spirit of offense will be broken in Jesus' name!

6

UNITY IS ESSENTIAL

As I was growing up my brother and I had a strained relationship. We fought often but we always fought fair and had some ground rules of how we fought. We were brothers but at times we seemed like enemies. It was not my brother's fault. I was mostly to blame. You see, I have always been a habitual agitator. When I worked for General Electric, the nickname I was given by my co-workers was "Maytag" because a Maytag is known for its agitator.

I remember the day my brother almost killed me. Eric was a big television watcher and, growing up, he loved watching his favorite shows. He didn't like anyone to bother him when they were on. My dad had this Ray Stevens album that contained a song called *In*

The Mood, The Chicken Version. My brother hated it and I knew it. So, now it was the middle of summer and my parents were at work, Eric was lying on the floor watching TV, when all of a sudden a thought popped in my head. "Play the chicken song". I don't know where the thought came from but I know it wasn't God. I decided to follow the voices.

I was blessed with an incredible stereo in my room as well as a lock on my door. I proceeded to play the chicken song at full volume not once not twice but for an hour. Eric was a patient teenager but after a while of being interrupted by the Chicken Song, the heat was on. I heard him at my door trying to get in. My heart was racing as if we were in a thriller movie. He was trying every way he could to get inside the door. He was beating, he was clawing, he was going to break the door down. Then fell a silence (except for the chicken song). Had I won? No, my brother returned with a way to pick the lock, and in a second, he was in the room. I was face to face with a madman that had just endured a grueling hour with the chickens. The rest was history. I was beat up, smitten, bruised, and left for dead. Well, maybe

I exaggerated that last part but I was beat up pretty good. By the way, I didn't play the chicken song anymore. Even I grew sick of it.

I lived in a house with my parents and my brother and we did not always have unity together. Therefore, it affected all the relationships in our family. We would get along at times but more often than not we hurt my parents by the way we bickered and fought. Church is a lot like family. Bickering or even just friction can divide the church.

Just as a family needs unity so does the church. *Webster's Dictionary* defines unity as the state of being one, being united, singleness, the quality of being one in spirit, harmony.

I have pastored three churches who have gone through major problems before I got there. Two had lost at least half its membership because of the division. Walking into these churches one could sense that there had been a major breach in the unity. You could literally sense it! We understand that only time heals these things but shouldn't unity be a byproduct of the church?

One person I interviewed shared with me how she felt during the heat of a church battle.

She said, "I was a new member of this church when the pastor was voted out. Even though many of the members stayed at the church, I could feel a split in the congregation even though there wasn't a 'church split'. Befriending the pastor and his wife during the days before and after the election, or during a crisis in the church is important no matter how others are acting. Because of the division and bitterness I felt, I didn't feel like an actual member of this church until the new pastor and his family were elected."

This is often typical of church problems. Most people only have unity with those who think like them or are on their side. If someone agrees with their views, they are in harmony. If they disagree or do not take their side, they are outcasts.

The church in the book of Acts thrived because they were of one mind and one accord. They saw the outpouring of the Holy Spirit because of their singleness of mind. For any church to go forward it must be unified in one mind and one accord.

Acts 2:1, "When the day of Pentecost had fully

come, they were all with one accord in one place."

The church was in one accord. The phrase one accord means being unanimous, being in agreement, having one mind and purpose. This is the reason for the church's power. UNITY! Without unity the church will never reach the world for Christ.

We might wonder why the church fails in this area but the answer is that we have our focus on the wrong things. Our minds need to be on the things of God. In order for the church to go forward; we must have unity in several areas.

There must be Unity In Purpose

In Philippians 1:27, Paul tells the Philippian believers that they should strive together with the gospel of Christ in mind.

Paul writes, "Only let your conduct be worthy of the gospel of Christ...that you stand fast in one spirit, with one mind striving together for the faith of the gospel,"

Every believer should be unified in the purpose of promoting the gospel of Christ. Our common purpose is building the Kingdom of

God. If this is our goal, we will not be worried about our own kingdoms.

The reason many churches divide is because people have little purpose. The old adage tells us, "An idle mind is the devil's workshop." If we do not have a common goal, we will be going in separate directions. We must take into account that in every church there are two different types of people: The *busy person* who is working for the kingdom of God and living in harmony with others. The *busybody* who goes around without a purpose and distracts everyone else from their purpose. Which one of these are you? A busy person or a busybody?

There must be unity in prayer.

When we know our purpose, our prayer will have focus. The early church prayed in one accord. They all had the same mind and were praying for the same thing. They prayed together for God to work among them and through them. They prayed for the outpouring of the Holy Spirit. This is what their minds were focused on.

I have witnessed in the churches I have pastored that the common denominator for overcoming division was not programs but rather prayer. It has made a tremendous difference in the atmosphere and relationship within the church. The more you pray for someone else, the more unified you will become with them. It is hard to pray for someone frequently and not grow to love them. The goal of prayer is to draw us closer to God and to our brothers and sisters in Christ.

There must be unity in worship.

In the book of II Chronicles there is an awesome scripture that is an example of unity in worship.

II Chronicles 5:13, "indeed it came to pass, when the trumpeters and singers were as one, to make one sound to be heard praising and thanking the Lord, and when they lifted up their voice with the trumpets and cymbals and instruments of music, and praised the Lord, saying 'for He is good, for His mercy endures forever,' that the house, the house of the Lord was filled with a cloud, so that the priests could not continue ministering because of the cloud; for the glory of the Lord filled the house of God."

Can you imagine this setting? The singers and musicians were as one. You could not tell one from the other because they were in such harmony. The Israelites had left their differences at the door and became unified in their worship.

Think about how God feels when we sing a song to Him in a church service, yet we have hard feelings toward someone else in the church. In fact, worship itself is a source of division in the church. Should we be charismatic or conservative? Should we sing choruses or hymns? Should we allow a full band or just stick with the piano or organ? Believe it or not, these are all major causes of division in some churches.

The Hartford Institute of Religion discovered that 15.6 percent of church problems were caused by this issue - worship. Something that was meant to glorify God and please Him ends up dividing a great deal of churches. It is not about the songs we sing or the way we sing them or even the way we worship as much as it is about the heart of it.

Jesus said that we should worship God in Spirit and in truth. This simply means in the purity of heart more than the method. Our voices should be as one as we worship the Lamb of Glory. God wants the church to worship Him in one accord.

We must have unity in supporting the leaders of the church.

There is a verse in the 30th chapter of II Chronicles that shares the attitude of the children of Judah to their leaders. *It reads, "Also the hand of God was on Judah to give them singleness of heart to obey the command of the king and the leaders, at the word of the Lord."*

Division often comes because of disagreements with the leadership of the church; 19.2% of churches said they had division because of decision-making. Why is this? It is because there are many people who want to be the decision makers. They must come to the place that we learn to trust the decisions of those leading the church and in turn put aside the petty factions that come because we do not agree with the leader's decisions. Disagreements will come but we must have an open mind and try to understand from where the other side comes.

One thing that we, as pastors, must learn is to make sure that we are worthy of being followed. We have a calling to lead the flock but we must do it the right way. We must never lead with an iron fist but rather with the heart of the shepherd, loving people with an unselfish love and with the best interest of the church in mind. This will help maintain unity.

When we are unified, we will reap bountiful blessings in the church. God will be behind the church who is unified. The Bible tells us that where there is unity, the anointing of God will dwell.

Psalm 133:1-2 gives us a picture of unity and it's correlation with the anointing. *"Behold, how good and pleasant it is for brethren to dwell together in unity! It is like the precious oil upon the head, running down on the beard, the beard of Aaron, running down on the edge of his garments."*

It is good and pleasant to God when His people dwell together in harmony. This verse beautifully describes that it is like the oil that was poured over the priest's head for consecration. It would run down his face and drip off his beard. The oil is a symbol of the anointing of the Holy Spirit. It was the early church who experienced the outpouring of the Holy Spirit as a result of being in one mind and one accord.

God desires to saturate His church with a powerful anointing. He wants to pour out His Spirit upon us, but we hinder Him when we are not unified. When the church comes together and becomes one, the anointing of the Holy Spirit will flow. We will be saturated if we will be in one mind and one accord.

Another blessing of unity is that miracles happen when there is harmony.

Acts 5:12, "And through the hands of the apostles, many signs and wonders were done among the people. And they were all with one accord in Solomon's porch."

I would dare say that when we come together in unity we will see God perform miracles like we have never seen before.

The sky is the limit for a unified church. Remember the story of the tower of Babel being built? God had to stop this group of people who were trying to build a tower up to God. Why would God have to stop them?

Genesis 11:6, "and the Lord said, 'Indeed the people are one and they all have one language, and this is what they begin to do; now nothing that they propose to do will be withheld from them."

Nothing will be withheld from them because they spoke the same thing. They made up their minds and stuck to it. They were unified. God intervened and the tower never got finished but it does show the power of unity.

What would the church be like if we all spoke the same thing? What could we accomplish if we all had the same purpose in building God's Kingdom? The sky is the limit for the church that is in unity.

7

THE CROSS OR THE GALLOWS

It was a normal summer day in the South Texas heat. The temperature showed one hundred degrees outside. Nothing but the hot gulf breeze was blowing. For my nephews, it was another day cooped up in the house together because it was just too hot to go outside.

What is interesting about Michael and Jonathan is that they get along about as well as my brother and I did at eight and ten years old. Remember the chicken song? I don't know who started the fight, but tempers began to flare in the house.

Jonathan, the younger one, threw the first punch. He landed a good one on Michael. Michael then took over and proceeded to pound

Jonathan. Fortunately, before either one was killed, the fight was broken up by their mother. Both of them got in trouble and only a few scars were left behind.

When my mother found out about the fight, she had one of those good spiritual talks with Michael.

"Michael," she asked, "you got in trouble because you hit your brother, right?"

"Yes, but he hit me first, " Michael responded.

My mom declared, "Well, the Bible says that we are to turn the other cheek. That is what you should have done."

Michael, with all the wisdom he could muster up, said, "The Bible also says, 'Do unto others as you would have them do unto you.' Since Jonathan hit me first, I thought he wanted the same thing done to him."

Revenge is a natural tendency for all of us. Ingrained within our minds is a thought that we have the right to get even when someone hurts us. We are entitled to that. Right? Webster's defines revenge as to inflict damage, injury or punishment in return for an injury or insult. Because we have been hurt it is our tendency to

Gospel of Jesus Christ. At that moment, I took on a burden that I believe is shared with the heart of God, a burden for His great church.

There is no greater institution on earth than the church of Jesus Christ. There is not another organism that does as much good as God's great church. Through the years, God's people have promoted the gospel to the entire world. It is this movement that is among the first responders of tragedies and natural disasters. God's great church is a living being that blesses humanity with the gift of love and compassion.

It is also a family that embraces people from all social statuses and all walks of life. It is a tight knit family that centers around the heart of God and His work. We, as God's people, are striving to be made into His likeness and to follow His Word and His ways. This is the church I love. This is my burden.

Like any family, there are problems. Sadly, the church sometimes has issues. In the purest sense, the church is how God intended to extend the message of the Cross. It is His intent to lead men, women, boys and girls to a saving knowledge of Jesus Christ. This must be our primary goal. This is the hope of the world. However, when we take our focus off of that mission and pursue other want to hurt them back.

It may be with our words, our actions or our lack of conversation! We simply won't speak to them anymore. Revenge is not just a physical thing, but it can be done with the way we treat others after they hurt us.

Romans 12:17 gives us clear instruction concerning this. *Paul writes, "Repay no one evil for evil."* This verse in Romans begins a text that helps us in our dealings with others. It sets forth the principle that we do live in a sinful world, and therefore, hurts will come. Because of Adam and Eve's sin in the Garden of Eden, this world was introduced to evil. It wasn't long after the fall of man that Cain took revenge on his brother Abel and murdered him.

The Bible is full of troubled relationships: Jacob and Esau, King Saul's jealous rage toward David, and David's son, Absalom, being built up with pride, trying to dethrone his father. Even Solomon talked a great deal about fools in the book of Proverbs. All of these examples in the Word of God had to learn how to deal with other people.

Even now in our world it seems that people have gone crazy. A recent study showed that the majority of Americans believe people are getting ruder and meaner. If you want to live with hurt in your life, you do not have to go far to find it. Friend, the point I am trying to make is that in the world we live today you either have to take those who hurt you to the Cross or to the Gallows.

The gallows were the place that they hung criminals from in the 19th century. It was the place of payment for wrong. They were tried and taken to the Gallows to be hanged to death. That is often the place we take those who hurt us. We want to see them pay for the wrong they did.

The cross is the place Jesus took those who hurt Him. He died for them. He gave His life for them. He did not repay evil for evil.

Some time ago in Houston, a woman was convicted of what was termed "a passion killing". In other words she took revenge. The defense tried to get her off on the plea of temporary insanity because she was filled with rage towards her cheating husband. She tracked him to a motel in Houston where he was found in the parking lot with his mistress. The wife of this man was filled with indignation and proceeded to run over him with her car; not once but twice. Needless to say, he died. She took him to the gallows.

Another case is the story of the man who had only one son that was murdered by an area teenager. The man was stricken with incredible grief over the loss of his only child. His heart began to grow bitter until one day he realized it would do him no good to resent this young man who murdered his son. He made a decision that day to invest into that young man's life. Instead of being hateful, he visited the murderer in prison once a week. They formed a relationship that eventually saw the young man come to Christ.

The father of the murdered boy basically adopted the convicted killer and treated him as if he were his only son. He took him to the cross not the gallows.

Both are drastic cases of wounds and hurts and although this book is about church hurts we can see how it relates to us. The truth is, in the church in which you have been wounded, there are those whom you might like to also wound. It may not be with the same wounds in which you were wounded, but it might be those cutting remarks that you make. It might be the gossip that you spread about that person when you ask someone else to "pray" for him or her. Revenge comes in many different packages; nevertheless, you must take them to the Cross.

So how do you overcome and learn not to repay anyone evil for evil? The Word of God gives us clear instruction in dealing with others that have wounded you.

Romans 12:18 in the Amplified Bible reads, "If possible, as far as it depends on you, live at peace with everyone."

Paul understood that some people are just impossible to get along with. There are others who tend to wound you every time you turn around. The answer to dealing with them is to do the best you can. Paul said, "As much as depends on you." You can't make people treat you right. You cannot force people to stop wounding you. You can, however, have a different attitude that is more difficult to wound.

If you do your part by choosing the Cross and not the gallows, God will help you in dealing with them. It is called the development of patience. Patience is often a trait we do not like to develop in our lives. There are several ways that you can deal with impossible people and have patience with them.

You have to be slow to anger.

Proverbs 19:11, "The discretion of a man makes him slow to anger, and his glory is to overlook a transgression."

The Danny Cheney version says, "Do not wear your feelings on your sleeve." You cannot live life today by being upset over every little thing. There are people who get mad over every snide remark or dirty look. Life will be long and miserable for you if you cannot overlook transgression.

Stay silent.

Proverbs 26:4, "Do not answer a fool according to his folly, lest you also be like him."

Keep your distance from those who hurt you.

Proverbs 22:24-25, "Make no friendship with an angry man, and with a furious man do not go, lest you learn his ways and set a snare for your soul."

Did you know that God doesn't expect you to go around people who hurt you? You are not expected to be best friends with people who could care less about your feelings. If people continually hurt you, stay away from them. Be cordial with them when you see them but you do not have to invite them to your birthday party. Keep your distance. Remember, Paul said, "As much as depends on you, live at peace with all people." You do your best, even if it means you have to stay away.

I like the way Paul first tells us to do the best we can and then says do not avenge yourselves. He knew sometimes that we come to our breaking point. Have you ever been there?

Romans 12:19-20 in the Amplified Bible reads, "Beloved, never avenge yourselves, but leave the way open for [God's] wrath; for it is written, Vengeance is mine, I will repay (requite), says the Lord. But, if your enemy is hungry, feed him; if he is thirsty, give him drink; for by so doing you will heap burning coals upon his head."

If he is hungry, feed him? If he is thirsty, give him a drink? What? Has Paul gone crazy? Just to clarify here, in case you might be misunderstood, you cannot put ex-lax in your enemies' food or give them poison in their drink. (Just thought I would add that.) Paul is saying kill them with kindness.

Aurelius Antonius said, "The best sort of revenge is not to be like him who did the injury." People who hurt you will take joy in knowing they got the best of you, so just be kind. When you come to the breaking point, take your burdens to the Lord not to that person.

I believe that the way we react to all of these trials is because we try to handle them on our own. Peter said to cast all of your cares on Jesus for He cares for you. The place of wrath is not yours but God's. Vengeance is in the hands of God. It is better to let God deal with offenders than you taking it out on them and risking sin.

Proverbs 24:29 says, "Do not say, I will do to him just as he has done to me, I will render to him according to his work."

If you are a Christian you have to learn to respond in love, even in times of insult. Isn't that what Jesus did?

When I think of our dealings with others I can't help to think how Christ dealt with the offenders. He walked with His twelve disciples for 3 ½ years. He taught them, invested in them, prayed for them, fed them and blessed them. In His greatest hour of need, they all forsook Him. Peter denied Him. Judas betrayed Him.

The psalmist records a prophecy about this. *Psalm 55:12-14, "For it is not an enemy who reproaches me; then I could bear it. Nor is it one who hates me who has exalted himself against me; then I could hide from him. But it was you a man my equal; my companion and my acquaintance. We took sweet counsel together, and walked to the house of God in the throng."*

I would dare say that it would be easier to handle hurts at the hands of an unbeliever but not your brother or sister in Christ. Furthermore, while hanging on the cross, those Christ was dying for mocked Him. The guards spit on Him, ripped out His beard and beat Him within an inch of death. Yet, He still chose to die for them.

Those are major wounds to bear but Jesus was just practicing what He preached. In Luke 6:27-29, Jesus gives us a five-fold remedy for overcoming the wounds of our offender.

"But I say to you who hear: Love your enemies, do good to those who hate you, [28] bless those who curse you, and pray for those who spitefully use you. [29] To him who strikes you on the one cheek, offer the other also. And from him who takes away your cloak, do not withhold your tunic either." Luke 6:27-29

Love your enemies.

The love Jesus is referring to is the same love God showed towards us in John 3:16. "For God so loved the world that He gave...". We are told that we must love our enemies the same way. You must love your enemies the same way Christ loved you when you hurt Him. According to the Bible, we were once God's enemies.

Romans 5:10 tells us, "For if when we were enemies we were reconciled to God through His Son, much more having been reconciled, we shall be saved by His life."

He loved us even when we were His enemies. So we too should love our enemies.

Do good to those who hate you.

Have you ever noticed that those who hate you will look to you for a friend when they need you. In one of our churches we had a young couple who didn't care for us. The young woman was filled with hatred and would backbite and slander us to as many as would listen. When we would see them they would just glare at us. The day came, however, that they needed us. Their daughter was terribly sick and they needed the pastor to pray.

I could have said, "No, you made your bed and now you lie in it. Don't trash me and then call me to pray for you." Instead, I said, "I'll be right over." I prayed for that child, I prayed for that family. I had to do good to those who hate me. After their baby was well, the confrontations continued and they finally left the church, but I always did good to them. You never know if your good deeds toward them will win them. Sometimes it does; sometimes it doesn't.

Bless those who curse you.

Bless in the Greek means speak well of, praise, extol, bless abundantly. This deals with how you talk about your enemies. The number one way we take revenge is by talking bad about them. It is a natural tendency but it breeds bitterness within your heart. When you talk about it, it doesn't make you feel better. It usually makes you angrier and angrier. Instead of speaking negatively against those who hurt you, compliment them. Speak well of them. This may be difficult but in doing this you will not hold contempt for them in your heart.

Pray for those who spitefully use you.

Take them to the Cross not the Gallows. Ask God to deal with them as He wills. Ask Him to change them. Don't ask God to kill them but to change them. A pastor friend of mine once said that he prayed two ways for the troublemakers in his church. "Lord, either remove them or kill them." He was joking when he said it, but we sometimes have that attitude. The way you develop love for your offender is by praying for them, asking God to bless them.

We must turn the other cheek.

Even when they spread lies about you or hurt you, don't react in revenge. Walk away from it and do the other things Jesus said to do.

We must not react to insult with injury. We must choose to take those who hurt us to the Cross. Imagine Christ standing right before you and that person that hurt you is next to you. You can either turn that person away from Christ or turn him to Christ. Even if those people are already believers, you still have to turn them over to the Lord. "Vengeance is mine, " says the Lord, "I will repay."

8

YOU MUST FORGIVE

As a pastor, I serve in many different roles from preacher to administrator, from care pastor to spiritual guide. There is one role that I fill that helps me understand people and what people are dealing with. This is when I wear the hat of counselor. When you look out over a crowd at church, you don't always know the history or pain that people have endured in their lives. Better yet, it is often in a counseling situation that I learn about why the unchurched no longer attend church.

I remember a time when I was to perform two weddings within a six-week period. This meant that my pre-marital counseling sessions would overlap at times. Rarely are two counseling situations the same. Most people don't share the same story. My goal for pre-marital counseling is always to introduce people to Jesus Christ and make sure they are in a committed relationship with Him before they make a life-long commitment with their spouse. I believe Christ is the anchor for any marriage.

Therefore, I always begin the discussion with the challenge, "I want to encourage you to make sure that you have made a commitment to follow Christ and make Him the central part of your life and marriage." Generally, there is no opposition when I say this, but in the pre-marital sessions I was engaged in, the next challenge met with resistance. I admonished both couples, "Every married couple needs a support system and the greatest place for that, outside of family, is the church. I want to encourage you to get plugged in and raise your family in church."

The response was the same in both sessions. Eyes disengaged and looked at the floor. They shook their head and stopped talking. "I'm not big on church. Not after what I have been through," was the reply. In both cases, what these couples had endured from the hands of believers was unimaginable. My mind couldn't comprehend how they were still able to say that they had trusted their lives to Jesus Christ. They loved Jesus but not His church. The pain that they had endured didn't drive them away from the faith. It drove them away from the church.

It was from this experience that I understood that *Sometimes, Church Hurts* and sometimes, it hurts bad. Every situation is different. Many times, it is pastors or ministers that have been anything but a man or woman of God. They have abused power and, driven by ego, divided the flock. Many times, our wounds come from the hands of another believer. We feel betrayed by the church and sometimes it leads to our faith being shattered.

There is a great deal of hurt that I have witnessed in the churches I have pastored. It is a festered wound that continues to be reopened in people's lives. The reality of it all is that no matter what you have endured, whether at the hand of a pastor or at the hand of another Christian, you must forgive!

My answer to these young couples was the same as I am telling you. No matter what, you must forgive. You will never forget the hurt, but you can forgive the one who hurt you.

It is never easy to approach this subject, because it seems calloused and cold. I am mindful of how harsh the pain can be. I have been there. I am only teaching you what I have learned for myself. No one is worth going to Hell over. Many people today have chosen to walk in bitterness and risk going to Hell over someone else's actions. I have made a decision in my life that there is no one in this world worth going to Hell over.

Jesus said, "For if you forgive men their trespasses, your Heavenly Father will forgive you. But if you do not forgive their trespasses, neither will your Father forgive your trespasses." Matthew 6:14-15

Forgiveness is not optional! If you won't forgive you will not be forgiven. He that shows mercy will find mercy.

I have been faced with many situations in my life where it would have been easy to hold a grudge. People have said hurtful things that have wounded me deeply. I chose, however, to be the better man. I forgave them! Well, most of them.

Many years ago, we had to make some tough decisions as a church. The board and I worked for months to come to a solution but we all knew that it would come with a price. When people are steeped in tradition, even a well thought out decision can bring opposition. We prayed for months, asking the Holy Spirit to lead us and we decided to move forward with our decision by planning a meeting to discuss it with the rest of our church leadership.

During this meeting we discussed our decision which was to shut down one of our major ministries for four months so that we could revitalize it. Since a certain member of our church was a part of that ministry, she was offended that we decided to shut down "her" ministry. She had been my antagonist since I first came to the church. Every decision I made was met with resistance because she thought she knew what was better for the church than I did. Slowly, I was developing a hatred for this woman.

In the meeting, she took me to task in front of the other attendees. She berated me and tried to humiliate me in front of the crowd, seeking to draw me into an argument. I chose to refrain from arguing.

Directly after the meeting was our regularly scheduled prayer meeting. I knelt at the altar and prayed. I needed prayer. I had to pull myself together to preach in just a few minutes. I felt someone kneel next to me and put an arm around me. It was the member who had disrupted the meeting. She knelt down to apologize to me. "I was wrong in the way I acted. Will you forgive me?" she cried. I was astounded! She had never apologized before. I replied that certainly I would forgive her.

As was often our custom, after the service that night, many of our church members gathered in the foyer and fellowshipped. The atmosphere was jovial, when this same woman approached my son, Josh, who was about 11 at the time. She was his Sunday School teacher. Angrily, she said, "Josh, what do you think about your dad shutting down Sunday School? He won't let me teach you anymore."

You can mess with me but don't mess with my kid. I could feel my blood boiling. Josh was stunned. He just looked at me and said to her, "It will only be for a few months."

For me, this was the last straw. I said nothing

to her. Nothing! I did not want to blow up in front of all these people. Sometimes, looking weak is better than looking like a fool. I called her the next morning and met with her to discuss it. We came to a mutual understanding but my heart was as bitter as it had ever been. I hated her more than ever.

I can tell you honestly that my soul was in danger. I didn't want to forgive her. I was fine at that point to live with hatred. She had wounded my family and me again and I would not let it go this time.

The challenge for the wounded believer is that the Bible does not allow you to live with hatred and unforgiveness. There is a great parable that Jesus shared that deals with this very thing. It is found in Matthew 18 and I like the way THE MESSAGE Bible translates it.

At that point Peter got up the nerve to ask, "Master, how many times do I forgive a brother or sister who hurts me? Seven?"

Jesus replied, "Seven! Hardly. Try seventy times seven.

"The kingdom of God is like a king who decided to square accounts with his servants. As he got under

way, one servant was brought before him who had run up a debt of a hundred thousand dollars. He couldn't pay up, so the king ordered the man, along with his wife, children, and goods, to be auctioned off at the slave market.

"The poor wretch threw himself at the king's feet and begged, 'Give me a chance and I'll pay it all back.' Touched by his plea, the king let him off, erasing the debt.

"The servant was no sooner out of the room when he came upon one of his fellow servants who owed him ten dollars. He seized him by the throat and demanded, 'Pay up. Now!'

"The poor wretch threw himself down and begged, 'Give me a chance and I'll pay it all back.' But he wouldn't do it. He had him arrested and put in jail until the debt was paid. When the other servants saw this going on, they were outraged and brought a detailed report to the king.

"The king summoned the man and said, 'You evil servant! I forgave your entire debt when you begged me for mercy. Shouldn't you be compelled to be merciful to your fellow servant who asked for mercy?' The king was furious and put the screws to the man until he paid back his entire debt. And that's exactly what my Father in heaven is going to do to *each one of you who doesn't forgive unconditionally anyone who asks for mercy." (Matthew 18:19-35 THE MESSAGE)*

Peter asked Jesus, "Lord, how often shall my brother sin against me, and I forgive him? Up to seven times?" What a marvelous question!

Notice Peter says it was his brother that sinned against him. Take that a step further. It was a Christian brother who was the repeat offender. Shall I forgive him up to seven times? This person Peter was thinking of was continually sinning against him. Do you know anyone like that?

Are there people sitting in your church that have repeatedly hurt you? Their words are like daggers piercing your soul. Their actions are nowhere near the righteousness in which we know we are supposed to be walking. They have treated you worse than someone in the world would treat you. How often should you forgive?

Jesus said, "I do not say to you, up to seven times, but up to seventy times seven."

What! Was Jesus crazy? Certainly He wasn't dealing with the people that you are dealing with. If He would only have to face the ones that you have to face every day He would have reconsidered that statement! If He only knew these people like you did, He would never ask you to forgive them, Right?

Hebrews 4:15, "For we do not have a High Priest who cannot sympathize with our weaknesses, but was in all points tempted as we are, yet without sin."

Jesus dealt with the same kind of people; yet, He remained without sin. In fact, the very ones who crucified Him, He pleaded for their forgiveness. Looking over the crowd of mockers on the Cross of Calvary Jesus cried out, "Father forgive them for they know not what they do." That is mercy!

Forgiveness is not easy. I would never proclaim that. As a matter of fact, it is probably one of the most difficult things that you will ever do in your life. You have to make the decision that no matter what they have done to you, you must forgive them.

Many people still harbor unforgiveness towards a minister or church member that hurt them many years before. It is time to forgive. Life is too short to walk with an unforgiving heart. It will control you if you will let it.

The only way to forgive is by asking God to help you extend forgiveness to that person. Why should you forgive? Because you have been forgiven.

The parable that was earlier mentioned is a classic example of our attitude towards the offender. According to the Bible, it grieves God when we refuse to forgive. It is interesting to note that in the text dealing with grieving the Spirit it deals mostly with this very subject.

Ephesians 4:30-32, "And do not grieve the Holy Spirit of God, by whom you were sealed for the day of redemption. Let all bitterness, wrath, anger, clamor [loud quarrelling] and evil speaking be put away from you, with all malice. And be kind to one another, tenderhearted, FORGIVING ONE ANOTHER, just as God in Christ also forgave you."

All these things are products of unforgiveness. Paul ends his challenge by telling us how to deal with such things.

"Be kind to one another, tenderhearted. Forgiving one another, just as Christ forgave us."

That last one, for me, was a shot below the belt. Why did Paul have to throw that in there? Forgiving others just as Christ forgave us?

The ultimate price was paid for our forgiveness. Jesus gave His life to pay for the sins and forgiveness of people who didn't deserve it. But He did it anyway. You must forgive them even if they do not deserve it.

There is no special formula to forgiving others. It is simply releasing the offense from your heart. Choosing to let it go. Forgiveness in no way discounts the severity of your hurt. You may have endured things at the hand of another believer that are unimaginable, but you still must forgive.

In my research on church hurts a woman who had been through many church problems shared insight into how she never allowed unforgiveness to creep into her heart. This dear woman was not a pastor's wife nor a minister of the gospel. She was a layperson. Her insight was invaluable coming from the perspective of a layperson.

Allow me to share with you from her own words: "I will pray for the church and pastor and assistant pastor and deacons and elders and Sunday School teachers daily, asking the Holy Spirit to lead and to guide them in His perfect way and will, and to give them His vision for our church. I will daily ask the Lord to forgive me of my sins of omission and commission and ask Him for His guidance, confessing that I feel that I am a weak link in the church and to begin change in the church and revival with me. My heart's desire is to be used of God and I ask Jesus to open doors of service to me so that one day I can come bringing gifts to the King. I think we have to be 'spiritually tough' to be Christians and attend ANY church. Therefore, I will purpose in my heart to quit being so sensitive and overlook things others do or say that hurt my feelings, because it probably wasn't intentional anyway. If I do have a serious grievance, I pray about it but do not talk about it all over the church. I will try to remember to pray for those who left our church and be kind and loving to them when I see them. *I will STAY AND PRAY AND FIGHT in the Spirit for God to accomplish His work in the church. I will not leave out of discouragement but trust God to water me through the bad times."*

In this area of our Christian life it comes down to a decision that we have to make. Will we forgive or will we not forgive?

We must forgive!

9

LEARNING TO LOVE

In the classic Disney movie, *20,000 Leagues Under the Sea*, we find a man named Captain Nemo who is seeking revenge against the armies of the world because of something that happened in his younger life. He had secrets that a certain army wanted but he would not speak. To try to get him to talk they tortured his wife and son to death.

From that day on, Nemo set it in his mind that they would pay for this murder. He built a submarine that had the ability to sink warships without anyone noticing. For many years he had sunk warship after warship and killed multitudes of sailors.

One of the ships he sank had survivors that were stranded at sea and they happened to find his submarine as they floated in the ocean. They were taken captive and held aboard the Nautilus.

Captain Nemo befriended one captive, Professor Arranax, a man whose writings Nemo had studied. After another night of revenge, the exhausted Nemo lay on his couch and asked Professor Arranax, "Do you know the meaning of love?"

"Yes, I believe I do," replied the professor.

Nemo then responded, "But what you fail to understand is the power of hate. It can fill the heart as surely as love can."

Professor Arranax contested as he left the room, "I feel sorry for you. That is a bitter substitute."

Many people have allowed the bitter substitute of hate to fill their lives because of a hurt that has lived in their heart untouched. It is left alone to brew and fester like an infected wound. But just as hate fills the heart in a powerful way, so love can fill the same heart. Take note, however, that the two cannot dwell together.

The power of love can conquer the greatest of hates. Such was the case in my life. In my hatred for the church member I mentioned before, I went through a season where I tried to hate but the Holy Spirit kept working on me. God has a way of keeping mercy in your heart.

I watched this principle being played out in my own life. It never failed that when I wanted to hate the person who wounded me at church, I would be called to her bedside in the hospital and asked to pray for her. Talk about a tough job. Pray for the healing of the one who has been a thorn in your side. But this was God's plan. Do good to your enemies.

In the midst of this season of my life, I cried out to God to heal my wounds and help me to forgive. One night as I was in prayer, the Holy Spirit spoke to my heart a new way to pray. "Lord, give me a love for her. Help me to love her like you do." It was that prayer that changed my life. It was that prayer that saved my soul.

Something began to take place in my heart over the course of time. I began to love this saint of God. We found our relationship beginning to heal. I can't explain what happened but within just a couple of months praying for myself to love her, I truly loved her and the all hatred was gone.

Because I began to love her with God's love, it mended our relationship and she loved me genuinely. No, we never saw eye to eye but we didn't need to because love covers the difference.

The people of God could do so much to change humanity if we displayed true love. Paul reveals this as he writes to the Ephesian believers.

"That Christ may dwell in your hearts through faith; that you being rooted and grounded in love, may be able to comprehend with all the saints what is the width, and length and depth and height – to know the love of Christ which passes knowledge; that you may be filled with all the fullness of God. (Ephesians 3:17-19)

He challenges them to be rooted and grounded in love. To know the love of Christ. Paul speaks of the width, the depth, the height and the length of love. This is the love that we must know. To know means to understand, to recognize and it denotes the recognition of love by experience.

Therefore, since we have received love through our relationship with Christ, we are to display that same love in our lives. The love of Christ passes knowledge. It is more than knowing. It is showing! What does our love for others look like? Do we display the attributes of Christian love to others?

Again Paul writes about love, but this time he writes to the Corinthian church. The Corinthian church appeared to be the most spiritual. They spoke with tongues. They prophesied. They had to be close to God, right? Not exactly!

Paul begins I Corinthians 13 with a thought provoking dissertation.

"Though I speak with the tongues of men and of angels, but have not love, I have become sounding brass or a clanging cymbal. And though I have the gift of prophecy, and understand all mysteries and all knowledge, and though I have all faith, so that I could remove mountains, but have not love, I am nothing. And though I bestow all my goods to feed the poor, and though I give my body to be burned, but have not love, it profits me nothing." (I Corinthians 13:1-3)

Simply put, Paul says, "We can speak in tongues and prophesy more than anyone else but if we do not have love, we have nothing. We can even understand the mysteries of God and have faith to move mountains, but if there is no love, it is no good. All of us could feed the poor and give our lives as martyrs but if we have not love, we don't have a leg to stand on. The root of all of our ministry and lives must be love."

Love is the defining character of the believer's life. It is the essence of God. Paul does not leave us without knowledge of what love is. He in fact defines it clearly so that we would have no question about what it is. What are the traits of that love?

Love suffers long...

This means having patience with imperfect people. I believe it is fitting that Paul mentioned patience as the number one trait of love. We are to be patient with flawed people. Christ was patient with us wasn't He? The fact is we should be as patient with everyone else's mistakes as we are with our own.

Love is kind...

Kind means active in doing good. Love is extended by doing good to other people, even those who are your enemies. The Bible says that we are to love our enemies and do good to those who hurt us. Love is being kind to those who you don't think deserve it. Christ died for us even though we didn't deserve it.

Love does not envy...

This means that love is not possessive or competitive. It actually wants others to get ahead. We are a competitive society. We play to win. My wife refuses to play Monopoly with me because I am shrewd in my business. I won't let her out of her rent when she lands on my properties. I play to win!

Love, however, is not competitive. I didn't say we had to let others win but our motivations need to be held in check when it comes to Kingdom business. The sad truth that many churches are divided because of envy and competition for power. True love is not that way.

Love does not parade itself, love is not puffed up...

This means we do not treat others arrogantly. What is it in the body of Christ that makes us walk around as if we are God's gift to the church and His Kingdom?

One pastor I admire greatly is Todd Hudnall. For quite a few years he pastored a church of nearly 2,000 in Lufkin, Texas. I had the privilege of having lunch with him on one occasion to seek wisdom and counsel. Although he was quite influential in our denomination, he did not act arrogant or prideful. Rather, he was a man of humility. I had lunch with him one time and the next time I saw him he acted as if I were a life-long friend.

We were at a conference months after our meeting and he was talking with other pastors of large churches that were gathered around him. He spotted me in the distance, stopped his conversation with the others and sought me out. He embraced me and looked me in the eye and asked how things were going in my ministry. It is evident that Pastor Hudnall displays the fruit of love for others; a love that is not puffed up.

As you can tell that had an impact on my life. Think of the impact we can have on others if we would lay down our pride and love.

Love does not behave rudely...

This means we display manners and courtesy. How do you talk to the cashiers at Wal-Mart? What about that waiter that messes up on your order? How do you talk to the leaders over you or under you? What about that person at your church who offended you? Love does not behave rudely.

Love does not seek its own...

Love is unselfish. It means you are willing to give of yourself for other's gain. When our son Josh was young, this principle was tested. Josh wanted a Red Ryder BB Gun badly. He could taste it. It was all he would talk about for days. On the other hand, I wanted a new fishing rod. My wife had agreed to buy it for me come payday. I was pumped. Think of the big flounder that baby would pull in.

One day as my wife and I were eating lunch, I began to think of how Josh would respond if I bought that BB gun for him without his asking for it. My heart melted as I could imagine his face when he saw it for the first time. I decided the flounders could have a little longer to swim because I went down to the sporting goods store and walked two aisles past the fishing rods and picked up Josh's new Red Ryder BB gun. I even stocked him up on the artillery (BB's).

That day I decided love was unselfish. It did not seek its own.

Love is not provoked...

This means love is not irritable, touchy, rough, or hostile but it is graceful under pressure. I must admit I had to repent before I wrote this part. I am often irritable. A few seconds ago you thought I was the greatest dad in the world because of my unselfish love, but I am not all that. I often suffer from a disease called irritability disorder. It's scientific name is Crankiness.

Taking this part of love as a quality in our life will help us deal with hurts at the hands of other people. We must be graceful under pressure! When the heat is on, remember love is not provoked. When they take mean stabs at you, choose love rather than responding with hostility.

Love thinks no evil...

This means it does not keep an account of wrongs done to it; instead it erases resentments. Love does not remember when someone wrongs you. I know this is a recurring theme in this book but repetition is good for the soul. That is how the Bible was written. God is wanting us to get the picture here. We cannot keep an account of what others do wrong against us.

When we confess our sins, God forgives us and remembers them no more.

Psalm 103:12, "As far as the east is from the west, so far has he removed our transgressions from us."

As far as the east is from the west? Put down this book real quick and go find a world globe. Look for the East Pole and the West Pole. Can you find it? There is none. The distance from east to west has no starting or stopping point. The psalmist could have said, "As far as the north is from the south," but that would have been a measurable distance. East to West cannot truly be measured just like God's forgiveness cannot be measured.

If God loves us that way, we should show the same love to others. Remove their sins from your heart. Forget about them. Think no evil!

Love does not rejoice in iniquity but rejoices in truth...

Love looks for the good in people. We often base our love for others on what they can do for us. "I will love you if...". But love is not that way. Love looks for the best in others not the worst. Someone once said, "If you always look for the bad in people you will surely find it." Do not be suspicious. Love!

Love bears all things...

We must hold each other up in the Body of Christ. The very ones who hurt you may be hurting on the inside. Maybe you could take the step to try to mend their hearts. Bear their burden. We must love others enough to stand with them when their load is heavy.

Love believes all things...

This literally means that we believe the best about people and do not look at others suspiciously. Love believes all good things.

Have you ever noticed how easily we believe the bad about people even if we do not know if it is true? How many times have we heard something about someone else and we spread it around even if it may be false. "I don't know if it is true or not but I heard ...". I have never heard someone say this when he or she is talking about something good. We tend to spread the bad. Let us be a people that only speaks good of others. That is what true love is anyway.

Love hopes all things...

This means we never give up on people. How many people have we written off? I confess there have been times when I didn't want to trust people again. I wanted to give up on Christian people all together. That is not the way love is. It never gives up.

The greatest example of this type of love is my father-in-law, Larry. I am certainly glad my in-laws aren't outlaws. I remember the first time I met my father-in-law. I was coming over to meet my wife's parents for the first time. Granted you must realize that my wife, prior to me, dated the pastor's son for several years.

After they broke up, she was determined to find the furthest thing from God. Guess who she found? ME! I was excited about meeting my future in laws so I decided to spruce myself up real nice. I combed my shoulder length hair, and I got my ear pierced the second time just for the occasion. I put on my best T-shirt and my baggiest jeans. I polished my combat boots and there I went. I was dressed to kill or dressed to be killed.

I walked into the house and my father-in-law, who was about 6'2" and, at the time, was about 280 pounds. He shook my hand and asked me to sit on the couch. He talked with me and got to know me a little bit and told me nicely to take care of his daughter. Home run! He liked me. However, I didn't easily win over my mother-in-law. In a nutshell, when I left, she cried. "Why did Sonya have to pick a guy like him? I wanted her to marry a preacher," she said.

My father in law looked her in the eye and said, "Give him a chance; you never know what God can do with the boy." Was he ever right. A year later, my father-in-law invited me to church and I got saved in the middle of the service. Thank God that Larry had love that hoped all things. I am indebted to him forever for loving me and believing in me. Love believes the best.

Love endures all things...

This means love remains loyal until the end. Even when the closest ones to you have hurt you, you might remain a loyal friend but it doesn't mean you have to hang around them or take their abuse. It just means that your love does not change. You will love them no matter what. What a way for Paul to end the characteristics of love! Loyalty.

Paul finishes this picture of love that by summarizing what it does in our relationships. Love never fails. When words cannot win people over...love never fails. When that person has hurt you and your friendship seems to end...love never fails. When that loved one won't get right with God...love never fails.

Let love be the rule of your life. Fill your heart with the love of Christ. Let it be manifest in all you do. Love never fails!

10

CONFRONTING YOUR OFFENDER

In the classic animated film, *Toy Story*, a scene unfolds where Woody, the cowboy star of the show, is being crowded by a space toy, Buzz Lightyear. Woody plots to eliminate this new threat to his domain. One evening as Woody and Buzz are atop the desk in the room where they live, Woody has his chance to knock Buzz behind the desk where he cannot be found.

His plan backfires and he accidentally knocks Buzz out of the window, where he lands in the bushes below. However, Woody still appears to be proud of his accomplishment but there is only one problem; there was a witness to this toy crime. Now faced with an angry crowd of toys, Woody is confronted. It is reminiscent of the posse's of the old West; they were ready to hang him. Woody makes excuses and says it was an accident but they don't believe him. The crowd ask Rex, the meek dinosaur, if he believes Woody's story and he replies, "I don't like confrontations."

This is often our reaction as well. No one likes confrontations. It is never fun. However, it is necessary if you are going to overcome your wounds. Let me give you a disclaimer though. Not all situations require confrontation. If you can release forgiveness without confrontation, then just let it go. If, however, you feel it is necessary to confront your offender, then do it.

Never just sweep things under the rug if you are harboring bitterness. Many people will live with unforgiveness towards a person even when their offender is unaware that they offended someone. In this instance, confrontation may be necessary.

It is how we confront that is the issue here. I remember confrontation well when I was young. When someone hurt us, we would take action. I am reminded of one such incident of which I confronted my enemy.

John was a ruffian. He was a bully to me. Honestly, I think he was a bully because I was such a smart mouth, but that is beside the point. One day as I was passing through his yard minding my own business (and his) he jumped me and beat me up. Fortunately, someone broke up the fight before I got killed.

Because of my sin nature I decided to take revenge. Equipped with a dozen eggs, my friend and I were going to bomb the enemy. We unleashed our fury of eggs upon his house with many direct hits to the front door. Mission accomplished! The worst part is the story doesn't end there.

By the time I got back to my house, John's mom was on my front porch. Be sure your sin shall find you out. It just so happened that if anything went wrong in the neighborhood, just look for Danny. My dad, being the guy that he was, made my friend and I go down to John's house to clean up and apologize for our confrontation. John's mom asked why we did it and my friend replied, "Because no one likes your son and neither do we."

That is not a good way to confront your offender. Egging someone's house is never the answer, although it might make us feel better for the moment. There is a biblical way that we can confront others. If the church would employ this technique there would be less division and more unity.

Confrontation causes people to be accountable for their actions and will make them less likely to be a repeat offender.

Matthew 18:15-18 shows us what we are to do. It is a three-fold process that you can take.

If your brother offends you, go and tell him his fault between you and him alone.

This is seldom employed in church hurts because most people tell others before they tell the ones who hurt them. This is why Paul talked about evil speaking in Ephesians 4. You sin when you begin to spread around what people have done to offend you. It is slander and gossip for you to tell others without confronting the guilty party.

You do not give them a chance to repent before you cause others to think bad about them. Furthermore, you haven't allowed them to tell their side of the story. You assume that they are wrong and you are right.

This is where you truly test people's spiritual

character. If they are one to keep it to themselves and not tell anyone else one can see that they are full of God's love and mercy. If they are willing to go to their brother, they are a channel of God's forgiveness.

It is important for us to understand that when we confront others, we must always do it in love. Our hurt tends to cause us to lash back when we confront. The hardest thing that we will ever do is to confront someone without letting our negative emotions rule us.

Friend, your offender will not listen to you or hear what you have to say if you say it in anger or out of rage. It is likely that you may cry or get somewhat emotional but be cautious how you treat the offender. The greatest thing you can do is confront with a spirit of grace and love. You will be more likely to win offender that way.

If he will not hear you, take with you one or two more.

If you go to them alone and they will not repent, then take a couple other people with you. Now don't take the head of the gossip chain or someone who does not have a forgiving spirit. Take someone that is a mature believer who has good Christian character and go to them in love.

Often when confronted by more than one person they will seriously consider their offense. They will make an effort to work it out.

If he refuses to hear them, tell it to the church.

If they still refuse to hear, bring them before the church. Paul said that we should mark those who cause offense.

Romans 16:17, "Now I urge you, brethren, note those who cause divisions and offenses, contrary to the doctrine which you learned, and avoid them."

Someone that is this stubborn may need to be dealt with openly. A pastor that I know had a couple in his church that were continually causing problems. On many occasions he tried to deal with them but to no avail. He finally had enough with the division they were causing in the church.

As a last resort, one Sunday morning, he asked the couple to stand for all the congregation to see and he said, "See this couple. No one associate with them anymore.

They have caused division in the body and the Bible says to mark those who sow discord in the body."

They left the church after that. Many would say that is too harsh. But to an unrepentant couple there is no choice. People are just too often afraid to confront people who offend. Now understand, this is only to be done in extreme cases but sometimes it might be necessary.

This is the process of confrontation and it is not only about you forgiving them, but it is about restoration as well. If they have sinned, they need to be restored and find forgiveness, not only from you but from God as well. Jesus said, "If he hears, you have gained your brother."

11

RECONCILIATION

Many years ago I read an article from *Today's Pentecostal Evangel* that shared a great article on the subject of church reconciliation. Deann Alford writes, "Pastors of a North Texas church that has mended a 56-year split into two separate congregations believe that reconciliation is empowering members to do more together than they ever did apart."

The McKinney, Texas, Family Worship Center was a Full Gospel Assembly of God when it opened in 1935. Twelve years later half its members left over leadership differences. The departing members formed Southside Assembly of God, which later changed its name to DaySpring Christian Fellowship.

"It probably should have never happened,"

said Dalton Froman, DaySpring's pastor during the reconciliation. "Everyone would agree on that." But neither Froman nor Family Worship Center's Pastor Charlie Tuttle are prone to dwelling on the conflict that divided the church long ago.

Much has changed in the intervening half-century. McKinney, formerly a rural town, is now part of the Dallas-Fort Worth metro area. The split occurred when the few members who still remember it were children.

Last year, both churches voted unanimously to reunite and combine staffs. On November 16, the congregations merged. Froman became associate pastor. Media attention and word of mouth about the reconciliation have brought in curious visitors. In January the church registered a record-high attendance of 316. That Sunday, 11 people accepted Jesus as Savior. Family Worship Center has been growing during the past year and a half; in that time 95 people have made salvation decisions in regular Sunday and Wednesday services.

The reunited church is looking to fulfill a vision that both congregations sought but hadn't the wherewithal to do alone: to proclaim the gospel in the city's east side, which has largely missed the growth and prosperity of the rest of McKinney. Family Worship Center and DaySpring congregations found their giftings complementary. DaySpring had a youth band but no building; it had sold its building and was meeting in a school in the growth area of the city. Family Worship had a youth ministry but no band. It also had a building.

It's all been possible because of obedience to God's command to forgive.

"When reconciliation and healing flows, it creates a momentum that's greater than we are personally," Tuttle said. "It was the force of completion moving the church into a place where it had never been before."

"When we release forgiveness, it releases us to work in the city," Froman said."

For this church to take these steps meant that people were willing to lay down their own agendas to follow God's agenda. I would dare say that thousands of churches would merge, if they all took on this ministry of reconciliation.

My in-laws used to live in Katie, Oklahoma, a community of not more than 75 people. It is a wonderful country setting with rolling hills and thousands of acres of pasture land. It is quiet and people are generally friendly. There is, however, the most interesting sight. There are two different churches of the same denomination sitting two hundred yards apart. Somewhere there had to be a disagreement and split. Why wouldn't they reconcile their differences?

Pride often stands in the way of reconciliation. Reconciliation literally means adjustment of a difference. It is an example of two parties coming to a mutual agreement that there needs to be a change.

The ultimate example of reconciliation is seen in our salvation experience. We were separated from God and through the shed blood of Christ, reconciliation was made possible. In order for us to be reconciled with God, we had to agree of our need for Him. God already agreed to the deal. That is why He sent Jesus to die for us. Reconciliation was a mutual agreement between us and God and we adjusted our differences. We were made righteous through Him.

II Corinthians 5:18, "Now all things are of God, who has reconciled us to Himself through Jesus

Christ, and has given us the ministry of reconciliation."

Take this a step further, reconciled in the Greek means, to change, exchange, reestablish, restore relationships, make things right, remove an enmity. This is the ministry Paul says that we are called to. The ministry of reconciliation. Not only are we to reconcile lost people to Christ, we are also called to restore people to right relationships with each other.

Wouldn't the world be a better place if we all were in perfect harmony? People often look for a Utopia, a place where there is peace and harmony. This is not completely possible until Christ sets up His Kingdom, but we can be advocates of reconciliation between offended parties.

In writing to the Philippian believers, Paul encouraged them to take up the ministry of reconciliation with two women who were at odds with each other.

"I implore Euodia and I implore Syntyche to be of the same mind in the Lord. And I urge you also, true companion, help these women who labored with me

in the gospel, with Clement also, and the rest of my
fellow workers, whose names are in the Book of Life."
Philippians 4:2-3

I am not sure what was happening between these two women but there was definitely something wrong that was causing Paul to take notice from a distant place. These were not women who lived carnal lives. These were ones who had helped Paul spread the Gospel. They labored with him and many other leaders of the church. They were not just half-saved trouble-makers. They were godly women who allowed Satan to drive a wedge between them.

Notice, their disagreement not only affected them but the whole church as well. They needed reconciliation before the church took sides. Paul encourages the believers to step in and bring reconciliation. He said, "I urge you…help these women." The word is the same for us today. We must help bridge the gap in the church.

Think for a moment about the church you attend. Can you recall anyone with strained relationships? They may be friends of yours and you feel awkward knowing that you are a mutual friend of enemies. God has called you to the ministry of reconciliation.

God has called every believer to help restore right relationships. This means that we are to help right the wrongs and to be a channel of God's restoration. You are not reading this book by accident. He requires us to bring healing to division. You may be one of the divided parties but He has still called you to take the steps to reconcile.

In the book of Acts we find the Apostle Paul in a heated contention with another minister of the Gospel. Paul and Barnabas were ministry partners. Barnabas was the one who stood by Paul when others were afraid of him even after his conversion. Barnabas and Paul were inseparable in the work for God's kingdom.

Although these were great men of God, they were still human. Paul was ready to take a tour back through all the places they had preached together to see how the new churches were doing. But the Bible says that Barnabas was determined to take John Mark with them.

But Paul insisted that they should not take with them the one who had departed from them in

Pamphylia, and had not gone with them to the work. Then the contention became so sharp that they parted from one another. And so Barnabas took Mark and sailed to Cyprus. (Acts 15:38-39)

Paul had considered John Mark a deserter because he left them on a previous journey. Paul's rationale was, "If he wouldn't go with us on the last journey why take him on this one?" This was not a matter of forgiveness but rather it seemed Paul stood by principle. It is as if he gave the ultimatum to Barnabas, "It is either John Mark or me." The contention became heated and they parted ways. John Mark and Barnabas went one way and Paul and Silas went another way.

There are often contentious times that come to our Christian relationships but they must not keep us divided. God never said we would always agree. He just tells us that we must not let disagreements divide us. It would be a boring world if we all had the same opinions.

After a period of time, Paul reconciled with John Mark over this issue. He was willing to lay down the contention and restore their relationship.

Paul tells Timothy in II Timothy 4:11, "Get Mark and bring him with you, for he is useful to me for ministry."

Years before, Paul had no use for John Mark but now he was needed by Paul. It may have been that he proved his worth to Paul. Or it could have been that Barnabas helped bring reconciliation to their relationship. The reason for Paul's turn around could have been many different things but it all is rooted in the willingness to reconcile. They made an adjustment of differences.

You and I must do the same thing. Whether it is in our relationships or even looking as a third party in other people's relationships, we must be ministers of reconciliation and help heal the division in the church.

Paul gives a clear instruction to the Philippians on how to reconcile. It is a simple one-point project. "Help them be of the same mind." The old phrase, "great minds think alike" is very true but it is highly difficult to make this happen. However, it is possible when God is included in the equation.

If we will get people to focus on the common

purpose of the church and its ministry we will see them think alike. If we can draw their attention away from their disagreements and focus it on God's Word, we will see them have one mind. Reconciliation begins when we get people to think of more than their own opinions and think on God's opinions. It is laying down our pride and walking in humility. It may even mean admitting that we are wrong, God forbid! Reconciliation is the only hope for a divided church. Will you be a minister of reconciliation?

12

YOU CAN TRUST AGAIN

He was a man that personified success in ministry. His life was an example to other pastors of how to grow a successful church. He was the picture perfect pastor. He could sing and was one of the best preachers in our denomination. His life embodied the success that most pastors crave. His church had blossomed to well over a thousand and continued to grow. Furthermore, he was reaching the city and souls were being saved by the hundreds through his many outreach programs.

Then his world fell apart! He had a moral failure. Just like that, everything he had worked to build came crashing down because of bad decisions. This pastor was caught in an affair with another woman, a relationship that lasted for six months. Regardless of success, no ministry can weather a moral failure without some casualties. Trust is broken and may never be regained.

How can you trust a pastor again after he has failed you like that? How can you trust another believer when that person has betrayed your trust and wounded you? The answers aren't easy to come up with but you must trust again.

Webster's Dictionary defines trust as firm belief or confidence in the honesty, integrity, reliability and justice of another person or thing. Trust is believing in people and having confidence that they are being honest in their integrity. But what happens when their honesty is really a lie? Then again, what if it wasn't a web full of lies, but one bad decision that led to their downfall? Often, we are wounded, not by deception, but by the failures of others. We are caught in the middle of leaders who didn't lead themselves. Sometimes these leaders aren't seeking to deceive their followers; they have just deceived themselves and, it not only affects them but affects us.

Trust is not always easy, especially, if you

have been hurt. In an earlier chapter I shared about a friend that I wounded. Looking back, I realize that the way he reacted was out of the emotions from another trust being broken. I discovered that in his life he had many trusts broken. The sad reality was that anyone he had gotten close to, hurt him. When I hurt him, it shattered part of his world because he thought that I would never wound him. He trusted me.

This scenario is magnified by the thousands in the church world. Trust after trust is broken. We have pastors hurting the sheep or sheep hurting other sheep. It may even be the sheep that are hurting the pastors. Whatever the case, trust is being trampled upon and few are able to overcome.

A church I recently visited while on vacation had a history of problems. The church had split many times but seemed to be well on the way to recovery. The pastor had been there for twelve years. The members had just built a new sanctuary. They were a church that was a model for a transition between tradition to contemporary. Something happened, however. All was not right there when we visited because, for some reason, it seemed a little out of order, not necessarily in a spiritual sense but you could just tell by the atmosphere of the church service. It seemed like something was going on.

Several weeks later, it all imploded. The music pastor was having an affair with the youth pastor's wife. The youth pastor's wife went to the pastor for counseling and the two of them had an affair. In all, three families were destroyed and the church was left with shattered trust.

These things sound like a soap opera, not the story of the church Jesus intended. For the success of any church, there must be trust in the pastor. Trust must also be with other believers. The problem is, that we get to the place of having to sleep with one eye open after all the things that have happened in the house of God.

Not only the preachers have betrayed trust but the laypeople also have. They have betrayed this trust not only with moral failures but with their actions. Is there anyone that you can trust anymore? Is there any way that we can find healing from these things?

The greatest advice that I can give you in this area is not to put all your stock in a man or a woman. Yes, you must trust, but do not put so much trust in these people that if they fall, you also fall. The classic example is the days of the tele-evangelist scandals of the 1980's. Several television evangelists were exposed for fraud and immorality and people that followed them were so wounded that they fell away from the faith.

You have to trust but you do not have to idolize. The pastor I spoke of in the beginning of this chapter was idolized by many. People followed him. They hung on his every word. They trusted him. To many he was the pastor that brought them to faith. He was the only pastor they ever knew. What now?

Psalm 146:3 puts it plainly, "Do not put your trust in princes, nor in a son of man, in whom there is no help."

The fact is, your faith has to be put in God first, not man. If our eyes are focused only on man, there will be times when we are disappointed. We have forgotten, as we have looked at ministers and spiritual giants, that they are still human. They still have issues.

They still have faults. The very ones that look super spiritual may not be all that they are cracked up to be.

That is where trust comes in. Your trust is in God first. Man may fail you but you can always trust God. Then, you trust man in a way that you are willing to build relationships and communion with him but remember, he still has faults.

The verse that says, *"For all have sinned and fall short of the glory of God"* is a reminder to us that everyone has faults. I am not excusing their failures. I know that they have the potential to devastate lives. Remember, however, the enemy is out to destroy the believer and the preacher. If we are not careful, he can destroy us.

If he can wreck your faith in man, he can hinder your faith in God. If the enemy can cause the pastor to fall away, he can cause you to fall away. Keep your eyes on Jesus. He will never fail. In the book of Psalms, David wrote over and over, "I put my trust in You, Lord." You must do the same.

I would dare say that the bulk of church problems is a breach of trust. Pastors who have been wounded by sheep somewhere in their ministry will not easily trust sheep again. Sheep that were wounded by a shepherd somewhere in their life have difficulty trusting a pastor again. Sheep that hurt sheep will create an atmosphere of friction in any church.

If you do not trust your pastor to lead you, your church will never grow. God has placed him over you for a reason - to build God's church. If you do not support his leadership because you are afraid of being hurt, you need to ask God to give you trust for your leader. If you trust God first, you can trust the pastor he placed over you. In turn, pastors must be men and women of integrity and humility. Furthermore, we are required to be servants to the body who can be trusted.

If you do not trust the other believers in your church because someone has hurt you before, your church cannot be what Christ intended. In many ways, we are building walls within the church house. It is a construction project that is taking place by people putting up walls in their lives. They will not let their guard down for a minute. They won't get close to anyone. They won't support the ministry because they can't trust. The walls that we build are insulated by fears. Fear of rejection. Fear of yet another wound. I cannot promise that if you trust again that you will never be hurt. I can promise, however, that if you put your hope and trust in God, you may be disappointed in man but you won't become a casualty.

This all goes along with the other chapters that teach you how to forgive and let go of the hurts. You will miss out on life if you are always suspicious of everyone and their motives.

Allow yourself to build relationships with others. Now, you do not have to allow yourself to get too close too fast, but you should seek out friendships. Then allow those relationships to grow. You never know what kind of friends you may find. The whole point is trust. You can trust again. Therefore, you need to take the first step and try.

13

FOSTERING HEALTHY CHURCH RELATIONSHIPS

The story is told of a gentleman who was lost at sea and became stranded on an uninhabited island in the South Pacific. While there he had to make the most of his time so he built, among other things, a hut. After being stranded for years, finally in the distance he noticed a passing ship. He made a fire hoping the smoke would catch their attention. Sure enough, they found him and began to make their way toward his lonely island. The crew boarded a life boat and paddled to shore and there they found a man with tattered clothes, scraggly hair and a long beard.

They were amazed at the places he had built - three finely built structures. They inquired of what each of them was. He said, "This one is my house. Here is my church where I worship every Sunday."

They looked at the other vacated building and asked, "So what is that one over there?"

His whole countenance changed as he grumpily replied, "Oh, that's where I used to go to church!"

We could be the only one in our church and we would still find some fault with it. Why? Because we are imperfect people. It is impossible to live life in such harmony that we never have disagreements or hurts. If all of us, however, would learn to work on our own lives and how we treat others, it would help us in all of our relationships.

Throughout this book, I have shared experiences that I have witnessed or faced personally. In looking back on the most painful of my relationships where I had to overcome hate, I came to a sobering reality. I was at fault in that relationship just as she was. No, I didn't humiliate or antagonize her but I did create barriers in our relationship and build a wall between us. I walked around with suspicion and because of that I would take anything she did as an attack. Much of that relationship would have been easier if we would have both given each other the benefit of the doubt.

We can all learn from our failed and hurtful relationships because church is full of them. So why don't we spend more time talking about how to foster healthy relationships? Because, sometimes, we don't know what to do or how to change. I have come to the realization that I can't change other people but I can change me. We know what we need to work on because the Bible talks a great deal about relationships. In fact, in the beginning chapters of the Bible, God said that it is not good for man to be alone. Though that is in the context of marriage, God places great value on all relationships.

Hebrews Chapter 13 also speaks a lot on the different relationships that we have - marriage, strangers, our relationship to the world - but it begins with church relationships. The author, under the inspiration of the Holy Spirit, starts it off by reminding us to let brotherly love continue. The Apostle Paul said that love never fails. Yet, it is one of those things on which we don't always like to rely. It's a challenge to love others even those within the church.

We spent a whole chapter on love so I won't belabor the point but I want to remind you that we are commanded to love one another, and it is that love which proves that we are Christ-followers.

John 13:34-35, "A new commandment I give to you, that you love one another; as I have loved you, that you also love one another. 35 By this all will know that you are My disciples, if you have love for one another."

Here Jesus tells us that all men will know that we are His disciples if we will love. People may see your good works and think of how great you are but it is love that shows that you are a true follower of Christ. So we must display love in every relationship, even the challenging ones.

Because the Bible speaks much about relationships we find in Hebrews the greatest scriptural reason for relationships. We need each other to grow in the Lord. WE NEED EACH OTHER.

Hebrews 10:24-25, "And let us consider one another in order to stir up love and good works,

25 not forsaking the assembling of ourselves together, as is the manner of some, but exhorting one another, and so much the more as you see the Day approaching."

Notice what the author says. Consider one another to stir up love and good works. He didn't say to stir one another up but to stir up love for one another. Big difference. He uses the word consider which means to consider attentively, to fix one's eyes upon. Stir up means to provoke denoting to provoke to love and good works. The writer says that we must be attentively interested in one another and provoke each other in the good things. Love and good works. This challenges us to help each other grow and pick each other up when we are down.

In a football game, you will see members of a team head-butting, hitting each other, or chest bumping in order to psyche each other up. When one of them gets tackled or falls to the ground, they extend their hand and help them up. The game of life is tough and we need someone to psyche us up so we can stay in the game. There are others who pick us up when we fall or are tripped up. This is why we need each other. This is the importance of church relationships. Life is too hard to go it alone and the church is a refuge for those who are weathering storms in their life.

The writer of Hebrews said that we are to exhort one another as we see the return of Christ approaching. To exhort literally means to encourage. The longer the world goes on, the harder life seems to get. Therefore, we need someone to exhort us and encourage us. This is why the church and the believers are so vital to our lives.

Sadly though, this is one of the hardest areas of the believer's life. We should all be encouragers but what about us? We have our own set of problems. It is hard to lift up others when we ourselves are beaten down. This is why there is often conflict or offense in the church. We all have our own frustrations and sometimes we take them out on others, even though we don't intend to. The reason is because we often lack certain relational skills.

God knew this was a common thing in church so He filled His Word full of instructions on how to overcome our relational difficulties.

He gives us wisdom in how to look beyond our frustrations and hurt and how to build lasting relationships within the Body of Christ.

In the fourth chapter of Peter's first letter, he gives us some wonderful insight into having lasting church relationships. He labels several things that will benefit the church if the members will adhere to certain instructions.

Fervent Love guarantees lasting relationships.

I Peter 4:8, "And above all things have fervent love for one another, for "love will cover a multitude of sins."

Fervent is a word that speaks of intensity and determination. It is an athletic term for stretching to reach the tape. Have you watched the sprinters who run the dash? When they come around that last turn and they're pressing for the tape, they'll get right to the end and then they'll lunge forward. We've even seen the runner, at the finish line, fall on the track, because she is pushing to reach the tape ahead of her opponent.

Peter uses this phrase fervent love to describe the idea of loving others being the same as that intensity at the tape. It requires stretching yourself, even extending to the uttermost in order to reach the love.

We must stretch ourselves to make sure that we love one another fervently. Peter says that fervent love covers a multitude of sins. He is referencing an old proverb here that describes the power of love. It is love that covers the sins of those who wound you. The word cover means to hide, to hinder knowledge of a thing. It denotes to pardon.

We find here the number one key to lasting relationships. Fervent love means overlooking faults, mistakes and even the sins of others. This is one of the hardest things you and I will ever do, especially if the hurts run deep or the sins of others affected us greatly. There is no way that love can cover the multitude of others' sin unless we are willing to display love and extend it to them.

In my years of pastoring, I have watched how on many occasions, people have overlooked the sins of fellow church members. I have even witnessed many occasions when saints of God have overlooked the mistakes that I have made.

I accepted my first pastorate when I was 24

years old. It was a small church in Daisetta, Texas in what I thought was the middle of nowhere. They were a wonderful group of people and were so gracious to me as I learned how to pastor.

It was a winter evening, about six months after I had become pastor and we were having a time of fellowship at the church. We were having a great time playing games, eating, and enjoying each other's company. I suddenly had this great idea that I would liven up the atmosphere. I have always loved to make people laugh and before I got saved, I enjoyed practical jokes. A quick lesson to pastors: Don't play practical jokes on your church members.

My son, who was two at the time, had brought his toy snake to church. I had confiscated it and put it in a place where he could not get it. My wife, however, should have hidden it from me. I grabbed the toy snake and walked over to one of our older members, who had previously confided in me that he didn't like snakes. Then, I dangled the toy serpent in front of his face. He started swinging and fighting at the snake. He was terrified and ran out of the building as the rest of the people were dead silent, looking at their 24-year-old pastor who had a sick sense of humor.

The man whom I scared was more gracious than I. He forgave me and never held it against me. Thank the Lord! If you are wondering why he was that petrified of a toy snake, it was because he woke up with a rattlesnake curled up next to his leg in bed one morning. MY BAD!

He displayed love that covered the multitude of my sins. If we are to make it through church, we must display this type of love that Peter talks about. We have to overlook faults. We cannot leave the church every time someone hurts us because we will never stay at any church very long. We have to learn to work through it or should I say, love through it.

Hospitality without grumbling guarantees lasting relationships.

I Peter 4:9, "Be hospitable to one another without grumbling."

This almost seems out of place. What does being hospitable have to do with church and lasting relationships. When you understand the wording here it makes all the difference. Hospitable means to be hospitable or generous. Grumbling means murmuring, secret displeasure that is not openly avowed, fussy discontent. This could be worded that we should be friendly without being fussy and complaining.

Peter is not saying that a person will never be cranky or that, from time to time, we will never be discontent about something. He is describing a person who is chronically like this. This is their disposition. It is a good idea to strive to always be friendly without complaining. Therefore, we must make sure that we don't let that define who we are.

Lasting relationships require being hospitable but especially without grumbling. How many of us like to be around a complainer? Do you like someone who grumbles all the time and is contentious? The key to having a lasting relationship is learning that grumbling and complaining to your friends only drives them away rather than holding them close.

We need to be encouraged at church rather than to hear negative things about others or the church. We need to be lifted up instead of having the flaws of others or the problems of the church pointed out to us. Be that person who will find the good in all things. Be friendly and hold back the complaining. Take your complaints to the Lord. He will help you overlook the things that bug you.

Personal ministry to one another guarantees lasting relationships.

I Peter 4:10, "As each one has received a gift, minister it to one another, as good stewards of the manifold grace of God."

Peter is on to something powerful here. When we focus on using our gifts to minister to others, we find that our relationships are strengthened and we see people in a different light. Peter uses the word minister here which literally means to serve one another. When we lay aside our differences, overlook faults and minister to someone's needs, God begins to move.

To think that God has gifted us is humbling in itself, but when we realize that He has gifted us to serve others in His body, we see His plan more clearly. He has gifted us to influence lives and furthermore, we can influence them positively or negatively. Ministry to others is a way that we can build strong church relationships. He has made us stewards of the grace of God. We are His extension of that. What it means to be a steward is that we are overseers of His grace.

This points us to the power of Peter's writing. When you minister to others, using the gifts God has given you, you find that ministry draws you together. I have found people easier to forgive and their faults easier to overlook when I am called upon to serve them.

I think of Jesus serving Judas Iscariot and washing His feet on the night of His betrayal. To me, that is the beauty of being a steward of the manifold grace of God. It is serving others who do not deserve it. Imagine that moment when Christ ministered to His disciples. While just a few hours later, every one of them would forsake Him. One would betray Him, another would deny Him and all of them would desert Him. Yet Christ's ministry on the Cross would bring all but one back. Ministry will bring people closer and will preserve lasting relationships.

Being unselfish guarantees lasting relationships.

Philippians 2:3, "Let nothing be done through selfish ambition or conceit, but in lowliness of mind let each esteem others better than himself."

Here is one of the most difficult elements of lasting relationships - having no agenda. Paul says to do nothing through selfish ambition. Selfish Ambition means electioneering and intriguing for office, a desire to put oneself forward. It describes someone looking to have his needs met without considering others in the relationship. It carries the idea of, "what can you do for me but don't ask me to do anything for you."

I had been out of high school for ten years when I received a call from one of my best friends in high school. I was excited to say the least. He had tracked me down and called to see how I was doing. This guy was a great witness to me in high school because he was a believer and I wasn't. We talked and caught up for about an hour and then it happened. I didn't suspect it nor did I think it was possible but selfish ambition came in. He was in multi-level marketing. He had heard that I had become a pastor which is a boon for these types of ventures and he wanted to help make me rich. What a good friend! He kept calling and having his network leader call me. They wouldn't leave me alone, and I finally told him not to call back.

One thing about selfish ambition, it doesn't take long to show through. This is the great destroyer of many friendships. When we have what Paul describes here, it requires that we have our way. If people do not bend to our needs, we are offended. When our interests aren't looked after, we get frustrated. Church relationships and church for that matter is better off without selfish ambition and conceit.

I have seen this on both sides of the fence: from the pulpit and the pew. Both the pastor and the church members must keep these things at bay. When we learn to walk, as Paul said, in lowliness we will have lasting relationships.

Lowliness means to have a humble opinion of oneself, a deep sense of one's littleness. This means that you find value in relationships and you do not think of yourself as better than others. Lowliness means we will lay down our interests to look after other's interests. It understands that we all have a part in Christ's body and one member is just as important as we are.

I can't remember where I found it or who the source is behind it but the Ten Commandments of Human Relations has been my guide for pastoring. It would do all of us well to live out the following commandments.

Ten Commandments of Human Relations
(Source Unknown)

1. Speak to people. There is nothing as nice as a cheerful word of greeting.

2. Smile at people. It takes seventy-two muscles to frown, only fourteen to smile.

3. Call people by name. Music to anyone's ears is the sound of his/her own name.

4. Be friendly and helpful.

5. Be cordial. Speak and act as if everything you do is genuinely a pleasure, and if it isn't, learn to make it so.

6. Be genuinely interested in people. You can like almost everybody if you try.

7. Be generous with praise, cautious with criticism.

8. Be considerate with the feelings of others. There are usually three sides to a controversy: yours, the other fellow's, and the right one.

9. Be alert to serve. What counts most in life is what we do for others.

10. Add to this a good sense of humor, a big dose of patience, and a dash of humility, and you will be rewarded manifold through life.

Church would be a better place if we all lived by these words.

14

GOD'S GREAT CHURCH IS WORTH IT

When Larry first came to our church, you could tell he was a broken man. With his young daughter in tow, he looked hurt, dejected and worn out. There was no joy evident in his life and honestly, he looked distrustfully at the appearance of happiness among the others who attended our church.

It wasn't long for us to notice a change in Larry. Little by little his guard began to come down. Smiles began to replace the distrust and now 2 years later he and his daughter have found a home at our church. This is their church.

A few months after he first attended, I mentioned to Larry that I was glad that he was attending and that I was thankful they were here.

I looked him in the eye and said, "You have a place here Larry."

As tears welled up in his eyes he responded, "You'll never know how much it means to hear that. I want to stay here if you'll let me."

Those words arrested my attention, "I want to stay here if you'll let me." Two things enter a pastor's mind when you hear words like that. First, "Oh no, he might be a trouble maker and was run out of another church." Or, "he has had a bad experience with church and has a story to tell." Something inside of me believed that he had a story.

Larry and I had lunch weeks later and I asked him about his life and his experience with church. He shared with me the heartache of going through a divorce and now raising a young daughter alone. He was facing many challenges trying to be both mom and dad but Larry has done an incredible job toting the load.

Larry had attended church regularly with his wife and daughter, as well as his wife's family. When the divorce was finalized he continued to attend the same church, however it became extremely difficult for him.

Of course, blood is thicker than water and he wasn't accepted the same by his former in-laws. The sad reality is that not only was he shunned by them but most of the other church members as well. Then the ultimate hurt happened. Still reeling from the pain of divorce, Larry was asked to leave the church. He was devastated and ready to give up on church.

That's when he showed up at our church. Someone invited him to attend our church and now, he has found a place. He is involved in a small group and is here every time the door is open. He is not the same person as he was. His wounds are healing and he is growing forward.

It was a decision for Larry to move ahead in spite of the hurt. He chose rather not to believe in "a" church but to believe in "the" church. The church is worth believing in. It is worth working through the pain to continue to find your place in the kingdom in spite of the potential for more hurts.

You see, this is the decision all of us must make. Will we give up on church because we have been hurt or will we work through it? Will we see the overall good of worshipping with other believers? This decision is critical.

Hurts can be overcome if we will remember that this is the church that Christ died for and the flawed people that make up the church are those that He sacrificed His life for. The truth is, we are all flawed and there is no better place for flawed people than church.

Therefore, for us to make it through tumultuous relationships, it requires living with the right perspectives. We have to live with a mind-set that overcomes the pains and wounds of God's house and sees the ultimate good of it all; to see that God's great church is worth it.

Time Heals Our Wounds.

Healing never happens overnight. In fact, it may require some time before you see your heart begin to mend but time itself is a healing agent. The sting wears off, the bitterness fades, the pain subsides and although we may have a scar, we find that we are able to move on from that offense.

In chapter two I mentioned a couple who had left our church because they couldn't overcome the years of hurt they had incurred. They had made the statement, "It is impossible to forgive." Truth is, it is impossible to forgive unless we have the help of Christ. God helped them find a church that would help in that process. They went there to hide in the crowd yet slowly they found their place there. They connected with others who were their age and they once again believed in the validity of God's great church.

After 2 years away, they believed that God was leading them back to our church; the church that had hurt them. The very place where they believed forgiveness was impossible now they called it home once again.

When they returned, they were not the same people. Joy had re-entered their lives. It was evident that their wound was healed and when they came back they began to serve in an even greater capacity. Time had healed their wound.

Don't Give Up On Church.

This is where many people end up. Needless casualties of the spiritual war that the enemy has waged against the church. People give up on the church. They associate their bad experiences with every house of worship. They believe the lies of the enemy that all churches are the same. But the devil is the father of all lies. He hates the church and wants to keep us from being a part of God's house.

When we give up on church, we give up on the greatest avenue for spiritual growth there is. We grow better when we are not walking alone. Therefore, we can't call it quits on church.

Recently, I befriended a young man who had been through some of the most horrific pains anyone could know. They were at the hand of a trusted member of the church he attended as a child. As a result, he checked out. He was done with church, the pain was obvious and he never cared to re-enter the doors of the church again. Through some opportunities to befriend him, I can now see that he is slowly coming around. He hadn't been to church in at least a decade but he is starting to come on an irregular basis. He is making great strides. He is finding that a handful of experiences do not have to define every church. Don't give up! Even if it is small steps toward re-engaging with a body of believers, take that first step and you'll find there is a place for you. Let God restore your faith in church.

Stay And Fight For The Good.

Let's face it, church can have some issues. After all, this book deals with the fact that *Sometimes, Church Hurts.* But if we all left the church every time there was a problem, we would never stay at a church very long.

This is often what happens. People don't get rooted because they are looking for the perfect church which is non-existent. I pastor the greatest church on the planet but we are not perfect. I am an imperfect pastor who happens to lead imperfect people. Parishioners may get testy from time to time and we may say hurtful words to one another or act unchristian periodically but that is because we are flawed.

Every one of us, have the potential to be hurt or to hurt others, yet we cannot run every time there is a conflict or our feelings get hurt. We have to stay and fight.

Through the years I have pastored some amazing people. Mine and Sonya's ministry has been to heal divided churches and even though it is difficult, it has been extremely rewarding. Looking back over these 19 years, it is not me or Sonya who is the hero, but the many saints who stood with the church through the test of time.

In our last church there were many people who had been members forty plus years. They had been through multiple church splits yet, they stuck it out.

I asked one gentleman why he stayed through it all and continued to serve in ministry in spite of the division. He said, "Pastor, there is no perfect church. If we all left every time something happened there would be no church here. I have stayed to support the church and the pastor and pray that the church can make it through this and impact the kingdom."

This should be the mindset of every believer. It is worth the fight.

You Need The Church And The Church Needs You.

I certainly believe that we are living in the days where the Lord's return is near. This is why the enemy fights against God's people and His church. If there is ever a day that we need the church it is today. We need to be among people of like faith. Those we can grow with, encourage and support when the times get tough.

Quoting again from the writer of Hebrews

who shared the benefit of the gathering of believers.

Hebrews 10:25, "not forsaking the assembling of ourselves together, as is the manner of some, but exhorting one another, and so much the more as you see the Day approaching."

We cannot forsake meeting together. You need the church because it is the place where everyone is going in the same direction and it is the place that you will find encouragement in a discouraging world. I cannot imagine life without the church.

The other side of the coin is, the church needs you. You are a vital part of what God desires to do in His church. You can be an encourager to others. You can serve to make God's house more effective in reaching souls for the Kingdom. You can pray for unity and growth in your church. The church needs you.

For the numerous people who have given up on church, there are many more who have chosen to work through the issues of conflict and offense. The majority find that God's great church is worth fighting for. It is worth persevering through difficult situations because this is the church that Christ died for.

God's great church is worth the fight. The good most certainly outweighs the bad. We need His church and His church needs us. Let's stand and fight for it.

CONTACT THE AUTHOR

To contact the author you can use the following means:

Danny Cheney
1710 W. Sycamore
Rogers Arkansas 72758

Email: danny@rogersag.com
Twitter: @dannycheney1
Web: www.lifeofapastor.com

We would love to hear from you!

Made in the USA
Charleston, SC
13 March 2015